Contents

ACKNOWLEDGEMENTS	
A Word from the Primate	3
Background of the Study	4
Purpose of the Study	6
Introductory Notes for Facilitators	7
1) What is a facilitator?	10
2) About small groups	14
3) Leading an adult learning group	16
4) What if conflict should arise in group discussions?	18
Session One: Responding to God's Call to be a community in Christ	21
Readings for Session Two: A Christian Context for Sexuality and Intimacy	28
What Science is Saying	30
Session Two: Seeking Understanding	33
Readings for Session Three: Sexual Orientation and the New Testament	40
Reading Some Biblical Passages often Associated with Homosexuality and Homosexual Relationships	42
Bible Readings	44
Session Three: Seeking Understanding in the Bible	47
Reading for Session Four: Conversation About Ethics with Tom Mabey	53
Session Four: Seeking Understanding in our Ethical Decisions	56
Reading for Session Five: An Exploration of Healing	69
Session Five: Living Out Our Baptismal Covenant	72
Session Six: Responding as a Community in Christ	79
Response Form: Our Message to the Church	85
Evaluation Form	86
Worship Resources	87

NOTICE

Additional resources have been prepared by the Homosexuality and Homosexual Relations Task Force and are available in one booklet from the national Resource Centre, 600 Jarvis Street, Toronto, Ontario M4Y 2J6. Phone: 416-924-9192. A reference copy is also available in your diocesan office.

The Contribution of Science to Understanding Homosexuality, by Dr. Donald Meen (for optional use with Session 2)

Understanding our Ethical Styles: Three Dimensions of Analysis, by Thomas Mabey (for optional use with Session 4)

Extended Bibliography, an annotated list of recent books and papers on all aspects of the subject.

1994
Anglican Book Centre
600 Jarvis Street
Toronto, Ontario
M4Y 2J6

Copyright © 1994 Anglican Church of Canada

Some prayers used in this study are copyright material taken from **A New Zealand Prayer Book — He Karakia Mihinare o Aotearoa** (1989) and are used with permission.

All Biblical texts are from the New Revised Standard Version (1989).

Canadian Cataloguing in Publication Data

Main entry under title:

Hearing diverse voices, seeking common ground : a program study on homosexuality and homosexual relationships

Supplement to a videocassette
ISBN 1-55126-112-X

1. Homosexuality - Religious aspects - Anglican Church of Canada.   2. Homosexuality - Religious aspects - Anglican Church of Canada - Problems, exercises, etc.   I. Anglican Church of Canada.

BR115.H6H4 1994   261.8'35766   C94-932401-9

A Word from the Primate

ACKNOWLEDGEMENTS

THE TASK FORCE ON HOMOSEXUALITY AND HOMOSEXUAL RELATIONSHIPS:
The Rt. Rev. Walter Asbil,
Diocese of Niagara

Ms. Sherry Coman,
Diocese of Toronto

The Rt. Rev. Jim Cruickshank,
Diocese of Cariboo

The Rev. Canon Helena-Rose Houldcroft (Chair), Diocese of Qu'Appelle

Ms. Diane Marshall,
Diocese of Toronto

The Rt. Rev. Peter Mason,
Diocese of Ontario

The Rev. Tom Mabey
(Ecumenical Partner), Nova Scotia

Dr. Donald Meen,
Diocese of New Westminister

The Rev. Dr. George Porter,
Diocese of Brandon

Mr. Norman Wesley,
Diocese of Moosonee

CONSULTANTS TO THE TASK FORCE
Janet Marshall Eibner
Susan Graham Walker

STAFF
The Ven. Jim Boyles,
General Secretary of General Synod
Paul Gibson
Joy Kennedy

OUR THANKS TO:
All those who have contributed their stories.
The Rev. Molly McGreevy for An Easter Story found in Session Four.
The Rev. Cheryl Kristolaitis and
Dr. Walter Deller for their contributions to the Notes for the Facilitators.
Doug Tindal, Director,
General Synod Communications.
Lisa Barry, Producer, Anglican Video,
General Synod Communications.
Dr. Terence L. Donaldson, The College of Emmanuel and St. Chad,
Saskatoon, Sask.
Saskia Rowley, Gordon Rowley,
Beach Graphics design studio.

The Anglican Church of Canada, like most churches in our society, is wrestling with issues of sexuality which call for ethical, moral and spiritual direction for our time. And among these issues is the issue of homosexuality and homosexual relationships.

The House of Bishops and others within the church have been addressing these matters for some time, but in 1992 our General Synod called for a study which would involve the people of the church in parishes and in dioceses. This study guide is an important part of our response to that call.

For many people in the church, as well as for many outside the church, this subject is new and even somewhat frightening. But the Church has in scripture and tradition much to say about the issues involved — sexuality, inclusiveness, justice. The research of recent years is also valuable.

But above all, at the heart of this discussion, there are persons, persons created in the image of God and redeemed by our Saviour's love, persons who are (sometimes unbeknownst to us) members of our own families and congregations.

So for all these reasons, I thank you for taking your part in helping the whole church discern the purposes of God for our time. The General Synod needs your prayerful participation.

May God bless you as you undertake this work.

+ Michael

Background of the Study

1976	In the summer of 1976 the House of Bishops commissioned a task force to provide an advisory document on homosexuality. The first draft was presented in 1977 and the document was submitted in 1978. The bishops made a statement in 1979 upholding the principle that Holy Matrimony is valid only between a man and a woman. Persons of homosexual orientation could be ordained but must commit themselves to a celibate lifestyle.
1985	In 1985 a study focusing on human sexuality and related issues of justice was presented to the House of Bishops. A study guide, *A Study Resource on Human Sexuality,* was made available to the wider church.
1987	In 1987 the House of Bishops issued a statement of concern with respect to AIDS and made a commitment to respond with educational resources and with pastoral sensitivity.
1991	In 1991 the House of Bishops upheld its 1979 statement. Also in that year the Human Rights Unit produced the resource, "Our Stories, Your Story", which was intended to help the wider church hear the voices of gay and lesbian people.
1992	In June of 1992 the General Synod of the Anglican Church of Canada decided to commission a study on homosexuality and homosexual relationships and referred its resolution to the House of Bishops. This study was to include:

- modern scientific knowledge;
- the Church's understanding of biblical teaching on homosexuality, inclusiveness, and justice;
- the experience of gay and lesbian people who are committed Christians;
- a report to be submitted to General Synod 1995 in a form that would be available to the whole church.

The House of Bishops met to consider this referral in November 1992, and in the spring of 1993 the National Executive Council appointed a task force to produce a program of study. The Task Force held its first meeting in October 1993. Because of the tight timeline it was decided to hire a consultant to facilitate the process. Janet Marshall Eibner and Susan Graham Walker were hired to share the consultant's role. Initially, the Task Force examined studies which had been done by other churches (to avoid "re-inventing the wheel"). However, in order to reflect the Canadian Anglican scene the Task Force agreed to design its own program of study using helpful components of other studies and sources.

Members of the Task Force reflect a variety of perspectives. They agreed to make decisions by consensus. The program of study represents the

BACKGROUND

convergence of diverse views, as well as the shared hope that the many voices and concerns to be found in the wider church have been brought together with respect.

Members of the Task Force hope that many members of the Anglican Church of Canada will participate in this study and will add their voices to help discern the "mind of the church."

The Rev. Canon Helena-Rose Houldcroft,
St. Philip's Church, Regina, Diocese of Qu'Appelle
for the Task Force on Homosexuality and Homosexual Relationships

Purpose of the Study

This program of study is intended to help members of our church engage in a dialogue regarding issues raised by homosexuality and homosexual relationships. We seek to listen to each other including gay and lesbian people; to the scriptures and to expert knowledge. By reflecting on what these say to us, our aim is not to propose solutions but to identify our diverse voices, and thus to form a context in which our church will be enabled to make decisions regarding its future.

This study is designed to:

- create an opportunity for deepening our communal experience as members together of the Body of Christ, by exploring our own feelings, attitudes, and beliefs;

- initiate a process of dialogue for members of our church to discuss openly and in love the issues surrounding homosexuality;

- encourage a safe environment for lesbian and gay people to participate and be heard as sisters and brothers for whom Christ died and rose again;

- stimulate a broad discussion of the meaning of the Gospel for human sexuality, open to a wide range of biblical, theological, ethical, and natural and social science understandings of homosexuality, and homosexual relationships;

- elicit the wisdom of our church to enable it to make informed and responsible decisions which will further include lesbian and gay people in the life of our community.

Introductory Notes for Facilitators

Welcome to **Hearing Diverse Voices, Seeking Common Ground: A program of study on homosexuality and homosexual relationships.** We commend you for taking on the important responsibility of leading this study and hope you find this guide helpful to your role.

This is a six session program of study. Each session will last approximately two hours. It provides a mix of Bible study, readings provided by members of the Task Force on Homosexuality and Homosexual Relationships, time for private reflection, and small and large group discussions.

The study is intended to promote dialogue and discussions of the heart. It is not meant to test anyone's expertise or to train experts. Rather, it is an opportunity to explore and test out how we are feeling and what we are thinking. As a facilitator you have the opportunity to model this as you work with your group. We know that the complex issues involved in a discussion about homosexuality and homosexual relationships can inspire strong feelings. However, we have learned, while testing this material in parishes throughout the country, that the program is reported to be more successful by the participants when the facilitator's own bias is not made evident during the course of the program. Another option would be to admit your bias at the beginning and then concentrate on the facilitator role.

DEADLINES FOR RESPONSES FOR GENERAL SYNOD 1995

For groups doing this study in Fall or Advent 1994, please send your messages back to the National Church (see Session Six) by **Monday, January 9, 1995**.

For groups doing this study in Winter or Lent 1995, please send your messages by **Monday, April 24, 1995**.

This will ensure that your group's considerations, thoughts and ideas will be part of the discussion at General Synod 1995.

Please send your messages to:

Task Force on Homosexuality and Homosexual Relationships
Anglican Church of Canada
600 Jarvis Street
Toronto, Ontario
M4Y 2J6

GETTING STARTED

We suggest that you distribute copies of the program of study to people who are interested in being part of this study as they sign up. These will provide prospective group members with some idea about the shape and content of the study.

FOR FACILITATORS

SMALL GROUPS – LARGE GROUPS

The process for each session makes use of time for private reflection, and both small and large groups for discussions. We encourage you to observe the process. Some of the participants will need to have some time to reflect on what they are thinking and feeling before they are able to share this with others. Some participants will only be comfortable sharing with one or two other people, while others will be able to jump right into a whole group discussion. In order to meet the variety of needs we have provided a mixture of groups. Sometimes, especially when the discussion is personal, we have suggested that people work in pairs. However, use your judgement about sizes of small groups. You might also want to vary sizes of small groups, through a session, sometimes pairs, sometimes groups of three or four, to provide a variety of experiences and good mixing of people.

REFLECTION PAGES AND FEEDBACK

You will notice that at the end of each session in this manual there is some space for group members to collect their reflections and ideas. We encourage you to encourage the participants to take some time and jot down a few notes between sessions. This will help them out when they are being asked to form their evaluation of the course and their message to General Synod in Session Six.

WORSHIP RESOURCES

Included in the supplementary material are a variety of prayers for use at the opening and closing of each session. Feel free to use these or others of your choosing. Perhaps you might also want to include some music.

THE VIDEO

You will need a VCR and TV each session. We suggest that you have the tape already in the VCR, cued to the appropriate spot before beginning each session.

The video and the manual are two parts of a whole. Neither is intended for use without the other. This is especially true for Session Two and Session Five which both contain video presentations of people telling their stories of experience as Canadian Anglicans who are gay and lesbian, or in one case, their story as a parent of a gay son. They are intended to be used in conjunction with the session outlines as you find them in this program of study. These stories have been given to us in trust that they will help us in our study. In return, we ask that you use them only within this context.

There is a brief video introduction to be played at the start of each session, where indicated in this manual.

For Facilitators

WHAT WE LEARNED IN TESTING THE PROGRAM OF STUDY

Group Standards

The **Group Standards for Enabling Caring Dialogue** is an important part of creating a safe and trusting environment for individuals to share their thoughts, feelings, and stories. We know that we need to be reminded of these. We strongly advise either posting your Group Standards on newsprint in the meeting room at each session or having them typed as a handout for inclusion in each participant's manual. In addition, for at least three sessions we would encourage that they be read aloud. Use your judgement as to whether or not it is important to continue reading the statement aloud after Session Three. Some groups during the test felt that the ritual of reading the statement at the gathering of each session was effective. Others reported that it felt contrived since the level of trust in the group was very high.

Reading Aloud

Participants found that reading aloud was a more helpful way of hearing the Bible texts and stories than reading them to oneself.

Guest Speakers

Some of the test sites were able to have gay and lesbian people speak with the group. You may have gay and/or lesbian participants in the group who are able to share their stories. Another option is to invite gay and lesbian people to come and speak to the group, especially in Session Five. This can be a powerful and effective supplement to the video.

Pastoral Care

There may be some times when it will be appropriate to offer pastoral care to people in the group. For some, this program of study might be a difficult or change-making process. For others it will provide the opportunity to disclose their own sexuality.

Before you begin the study, you may want to identify and recruit some people to be on stand-by, to provide pastoral care if and when needed.

Finally, make the sessions your own. Organize the sessions around supper meetings (a supper at the beginning of the study can help you get off to a good start), meet in participants' homes, do two sessions at a time on three Saturdays or Sunday afternoons... However, we encourage you to cover **all** the material in the order in which it is offered in the manual. In other words, the program of study takes, at minimum, 12 hours. Organize your meetings to suit your community.

1) What is a Facilitator?

A FACILITATOR IS A PERSON WHO:

- Is responsible for knowing the material of the program;
- Understands group process;
- Enables all who want to speak the opportunity to do so;
- Remembers that the Holy Spirit is always present.

A facilitator enjoys the opportunity of helping a group to listen to one another and, although uncertain of the outcome, trusts that the process will work. A facilitator is a person who does not attempt to answer all the questions but helps the group to locate appropriate resources, material, or people when they are needed. A facilitator values all the people in the group.

FACILITATOR ROLE — CONVENOR

AS CONVENOR THE FACILITATOR WILL:

- Create a sense of order and process for the session;
- Keep participants and the process on track by involving participants and keeping to the schedule;
- Use whatever resources are needed for clarification;
- Provide the opportunity for everyone to be heard;
- Summarize and/or record group discussions when appropriate.

FACILITATOR ROLE — NUTS AND BOLTS

THE FACILITATOR WILL:

- Be familiar with the content and process for the session;
- Be responsible for the set up of the meeting space;
- Be prepared to point out the location of rest rooms and telephones;
- Point out the need for attendance at all sessions;
- Point out the need to begin and end on time;
- Begin and end on time.

FOR FACILITATORS

FACILITATOR ROLE — SEEKING SUPPORT FROM THE GROUP

THE FACILITATOR WILL:

- Ask for clarification when comments or questions seem unclear
- Ask for help to get back on track when unsure of the direction of the discussion. *Example: We seem to be talking about something different, is this where we want to be or can we come back to it later?*
- Help the group understand that you share responsibility for the session
- Share leadership with participants by sharing responsibility for opening and closing worship, readings, and refreshments.

WHAT IF...

...THE GROUP BECOMES SILENT?

- Silence is okay — sometimes it takes time to think and respond. If the silence goes on for a long time, or people seem restless, you may want to restate the question or ask if the task is clear.

...SOMEONE IS DOMINATING THE DISCUSSION SO THAT YOU CAN'T MOVE ON?

- Create a 'parking lot' — a special piece of newsprint where concerns and comments outside the topic can be noted for later conversation.
- Ask the group if they feel that they are off track and need to move on.
- Suggest a break.

...SOMEONE IS HAVING TROUBLE GETTING INTO THE DISCUSSION?

- Watch for people who look like they might want to enter the conversation and invite them by name: *Jim, would you like to add something? Sue, do you have a question or comment?*
- Periodically, ask if everyone has had a chance to speak before the group moves on to a new topic.

...YOU FEEL THE SESSION COULD HAVE GONE BETTER?

- Take a few minutes at the end of the session to ask the group for help. *What could I/we have done differently to improve the session?*

...TOPICS AND ISSUES WHICH ARE NOT A PART OF THIS PROGRAM OF STUDY EMERGE STRONGLY?

- Suggest that the group include these concerns in the evaluation going back to the National Church through the Task Force on Homosexuality and Homosexual Relationships.
- Suggest that at the end of the course you might have an additional session together to discuss these issues.

THOUGHTS ON FACILITATING GOOD DISCUSSIONS

- Be clear about the purpose and goals of this study.
- Work from the session outlines and information given in this program of study.
- Encourage maximum participation. Avoid monopolies. But, respect the silence of those who choose to be silent.
- Be a careful, active listener.
- Think about the learners continuously.
- Give people time (pause and be quiet) to reflect on responses to questions.
- Help participants to clarify and/or extend their ideas.
- Move the discussion along.
- Don't impose your opinion or personal agenda on the group.
- Be prepared to rephrase or pose alternate questions to those suggested within this program of study to facilitate discussion.
- Be prepared to deal with disagreements in the group.
- Don't feel that you are required to resolve all disputes. Allow the group to help.
- Watch out for "red herrings": keep the group focused.
- Be patient and diplomatic in dealing with participants' more "off-the-wall" contributions. The group will help here as well.

THOUGHTS ON PRODUCTIVE GROUP DISCUSSIONS

- Everyone is clear about the purpose of the discussion.
- The discussion remains focused on the topic.
- One person speaks at a time.
- Ideas can be challenged without offence.
- People are listened to.
- Controversial and novel ideas are encouraged.
- Amiability and sense of humour are maintained.
- Discussion is not bogged down in seeking answers beyond the immediate ability and or knowledge of the group.
- Rather than asserting "rightness" and "wrongness", people accept that there are a variety of perspectives.
- At the end of the session, people are able to name something they have learned from another member of the group.
- The key points made during the discussion can be summarized at its conclusion.

For Facilitators 13

Thoughts on Summarizing and Recording

- Listen.
- Use the person's own words.
- Ask for repetition or clarification when you're not sure.
- Shorten phrases or find a word which collects several ideas.
- Check back to see if you've got it right, or if anything is missing.

Finally...

- Don't be anxious. You probably have the skills and gifts you need.
- Trust your instincts and trust the group.

2) About Small Groups

We have lots of experience being in groups. We belong to clubs, church groups, committees, sports teams, even our family is a small group. We belong to some groups for just a short period of time — to others for a very long time. We all know a lot about what goes on in groups from personal experience as members. We have had experiences in groups when they work well together, and also in groups which have not.

Here are a few tips you might find helpful to understand what makes a group work well.

EVERYONE IS IMPORTANT

A group is made of two or more people. Each person is important to the whole life of the group. We join groups when we believe that we can fulfil some need through talking, thinking, and acting together with other people.

Even when we think we know the other members of the group well, we will find a wide diversity of thoughts and feelings, backgrounds and experiences among the participants. This creates both great potential and challenge for any group.

GROUP NEEDS

Every healthy group has three needs present.

1] *Accomplishment*

Every group needs a task to accomplish, a goal to reach, a problem to solve. This sense of common goal is necessary. When the goal or task is unclear, the group will be uncomfortable.

2] *Relationships*

We need to be aware of how people relate to each other. Unless members really respect, listen to, and try to understand each other, the group will find it too difficult to continue existing as a group. The group standards that you will be developing in Session 1 are designed to meet this need.

3] *Recognition*

Each member of the group needs to know that their contribution is being valued. We come together into groups because of our needs for recognition, relationship achievement, new learning and experience. The onus is on the group to be sensitive to each of these needs in its members. We need to know that our desire to belong to the group is reciprocated by the group wanting us as a member. Decline in a sense of belonging results in a decline in a sense of responsibility towards the work of the group, and a decline of ownership in the group's success.

MEETING GROUP NEEDS

To achieve effectiveness and satisfaction, all three group needs must be met to some extent. Over a period of time there will be variations in the amount of group attention and energy directed to any one of these needs. The amount of attention will depend on what the group perceives as the most pressing need and their ability to respond.

One important way of meeting group needs is found in sharing leadership. Common sense tells us that no one person can always be attentive to the needs of the group. It is necessary to share this responsibility among the participants. Leadership is an active relationship between and among people in a group and can be shared among the members of a group.

If the group bogs down, a hint is to look for an unattended need and then respond to it or encourage someone else to respond. This skill of knowing what to say, when, and how, will come with practice.

For adults, an informal atmosphere makes for more and deeper learning. It encourages a free and full expression of ideas, opinions, and feelings. Each participant plays a part in creating this atmosphere by respecting the group standards.

3) Leading an Adult Learning Group

Think of every event as needing a Beginning, a Middle and an End. Here are some tips you may find helpful:

BEGINNING

- Beginning a session is about group-building — does everyone know everyone else?

- People need some time to set aside everything else and focus on learning together.

- Pray **after** introductions — some people feel very uncomfortable when they have no idea with whom they are praying.

- Catch up on learning since the last time you met. What's been happening in people's lives?

- A round-the-group question can help connect people — work at questions or exercises that will also connect with what's going to happen later.

- Remember that adults learn best when they feel open to trust others, to ask questions, to challenge assumptions, to share and weigh experiences. Clarify the group's norms and assumptions about confidentiality and criticism of people.

THE MIDDLE

- This is the time for content. Plan in chunks that give ample time for reflection, discussion and activity.

- Come with several alternative discussion questions and don't rush to abandon them.

- Use a flip chart or some other form of public record to recognize and document people's key ideas and suggestions.

- Groups need changes in energy. Changing the format of the conversation to smaller groups or pairs can help.

- Personal storytelling and sensitive material is often better left to pairs of people.

- Ten minutes in pairs is a fairly long time to talk together. Four people will take the same ten minutes just to get comfortable and started on the task.

- Art, drama, movement, and music all add energy to groups, and help people connect their feeling sides and their thinking sides.

FOR FACILITATORS

ENDING

- How well the closing of a group happens each time will directly influence how much people take away and are able to use in their lives.

- Clarify if there are follow-up responsibilities and tasks, and whose they are.

- Take time for prayer, reflection, and identifying what's been learned or valuable in the session.

- Use a few minutes for all the group to share the cleaning up tasks.

- Encourage feedback. Ask what people enjoyed, what they found challenging or difficult. Ask them what they would have done differently if they had been leading the session. Treat it as information that will help you develop a better session next time.

- Some physical ritual such as gathering in a circle around a candle, sharing the Grace, will help symbolize the togetherness of the group, as well as their breaking apart to move to other aspects of their lives.

By Dr. Walter Deller, Coordinator at the LOGOS Institute, Diocese of Toronto

These pages are excerpted from the LOGOS Newsletter in THE ANGLICAN, Diocese of Toronto, October 1993

4) What if Conflict Should Arise in Group Discussions?

Let's assume that not everyone is going to agree with one another when discussing homosexuality and homosexual relationships. After all, if we all had the same point of view, we wouldn't need this program of study. Knowing that there will be a variety of opinions, thoughts and feelings means that we can prepare for potential conflict before discussion begins.

SETTING THE TONE FOR THE GROUP BEFORE CONFLICT BEGINS IS CRUCIAL

- Developing rules, or group standards, means that everyone gets to decide what behaviour is acceptable.

- Deciding as a group how to deal with unacceptable behaviour, such as name-calling, is also important.

- Knowing how to communicate with one another — *"In this group we will listen to each other and not interrupt the speaker"* — also makes it easier for honest discussion to begin.

An important part of setting a tone for the group is talking about differences. Differences of approach and differences of opinion are part of what makes each of us a unique creation of God. If the group agrees that people can differ and still respect one another, then the basis for a good, honest discussion is set.

COMMUNICATING EFFECTIVELY WITH ONE ANOTHER DIFFUSES CONFLICT

No matter what group standards may be set, if members of the group do not listen to one another, misinterpret one another, or speak for one another, conflict will get worse. To help avoid this have the group members speak only of what *they* think or feel and avoid interpreting what others say. For example, if someone says, "People of all sexual orientations should be welcome at our church", another person, in responding to this could say, "Welcoming everybody would make me feel I have to abandon the moral standards I've been taught" rather than "You say we should welcome everyone because you don't understand what being Christian really means."

There are times when something negative might be said to someone. Receiving negative comments is an art in itself. When you receive a negative comment in a respectful manner, it goes a long way towards diffusing tension and creating mutual respect. You may wish to present the following points to the group and ask if they will agree to try to follow them.

IF YOU FEEL YOU ARE BEING CRITICIZED

- Make it clear that you are listening by looking directly at the person talking to you. Avoid moving backwards.
- Under no condition find fault with the person who has just criticized you.
- Don't imply that your critic has some ulterior or hostile motive.
- Be serious — don't jest, make fun, or caricature the complainant.
- Stay on the subject.
- Even though you may not agree with what your critic has said, let them know that you understand his/her objection. An effective way of doing this is to restate the main point of the complaint focusing on the issue not the person. For example, one participant accuses another of putting their children at risk by welcoming homosexual church school teachers. A response might be, "The idea of gay and lesbian people working with children really makes you anxious."

This all takes some practice. If a discussion becomes very hot and group members are breaking their own rules, the group leader or the group as a whole can call for a break. A break is designed to reduce tension. One way to do this is to have a one or two minute period of silence ending with a review of the group standards and a prayer for meeting together such as:

God our Creator,
when you speak there is light and life,
when you act there is justice and love;
grant that your love may be present in our meeting,
so that what we say and what we do
may be filled with your Holy Spirit.
Amen.

[from the *New Zealand Prayer Book*]

Or

We give you thanks, Spirit of Wisdom,

for you speak to us in ways that often surprise us.

You uncover truths that we have kept hidden from ourselves,

and support us in tasks we fear to undertake alone.

We give thanks for your invitations to growth and intimacy and fullness of life,

and for the comfort you extend in our often uphill struggle to be faithful. Amen.

[From *More Than Words* by Janet Schaffran and Pat Kozak]

Meeting together to discuss complex and challenging issues gives us an opportunity to discern what God wants for us as a community of faithful people. How we listen and respect one another is as important as what we decide to do in Christ's name.

The Rev. Cheryl Kristolaitis is an educator and writer living in North Bay, Ontario

Session One 21

1 Responding to God's call to be a community in Christ

OBJECTIVE:

To build the learning community. It is important to spend time getting acquainted in this setting even when the participants already know one another, to set other things aside and to focus on learning together.

Time: 45 minutes.

Introduce yourself as the facilitator, taking a few minutes to describe your role within the group and your reasons for leading the study.

Ask the participants to introduce themselves by name.

> **NEEDED FOR EACH SESSION**
>
> Name tags
>
> TV/VCR ready and cued with tape
>
> Opening and closing prayers (chosen from the worship resources or on newsprint)
>
> Questions you will be asking during the session on newsprint — ready to display when needed
>
> Some extra pencils
>
> Refreshments

SESSION GOALS

- To understand the purpose of this program of study.
- To subscribe to a set of group standards for enabling caring dialogue.
- To begin to explore the issues of homosexuality and homosexual relationships.

GATHERING:
MEETING FOR THE FIRST TIME

INTRODUCTIONS

OUR AGREEMENT ABOUT GROUP STANDARDS

WHY GROUP STANDARDS?

To create a safe environment. We will develop and subscribe to a set of group standards and agree to work within them during the course of this study so that:

- We are able to hear what others have to say;
- We feel that we can be heard;
- We can show respect for each other as members of the group.

Individual reflection.

Ask each participant to think of a hope and a fear they bring to this event.

Ask each participant to finish these sentences for themselves:

When all have finished writing, ask the participants to share their statements with the group. Record the statements on newsprint.

Ask participants to read **Group Standards For Enabling Caring Dialogue**

> Chances are you will run short of time. If this happens, delegate the task to a small group to work on the standards and present it at the beginning of the next session.
>
> OUR GROUP STANDARDS can then be written as a handout to be included with their study material or on newsprint to be posted and reviewed at each session.

DEVELOPING OUR GROUP STANDARDS

So that we can each work towards fulfilling our hopes and diminishing our fears:

As a member of this group I will...

As a group we will...

Using the **Group Standards For Enabling Caring Dialogue** and the participants' own statements from the newsprint, develop a set of standards for your group.

GROUP STANDARDS FOR ENABLING CARING DIALOGUE

We are gathered to engage in this program of study agreeing that:

- Our sessions are confidential. We pledge our confidentiality about what is said here; we will not discuss what anyone says, even with those closest to us.

- We are free to discuss our own comments or feelings with those outside this group, but not the comments and feelings of any other person in this group.

- We will speak only for ourselves, from our own experience, using 'I' statements. We will avoid generalizations.

- We will give each other time to speak and to be heard without interruption. Differing views will not be argued, but honoured as valid for that person.

- We will honour each person's right to express their own understanding or belief.

- We discuss issues. We do not name people.

SESSION ONE 23

- We have the freedom *not* to speak, *not* to get involved in a particular activity. We are responsible for our own feelings.
- We will take care that those who choose to reveal their sexual orientation to us are treated with respect and dignity.

FINISHING OUR INTRODUCTIONS

Ask each participant to say in one sentence:

Why I chose to come to this study

Prayer

(say together)

Almighty God, who created us male and female and who calls us to share in the creative and reconciling power of your love; grant that through this program of study we may come to know your will for us as sexual creatures, so that all we say and do may show forth the power of your love in our lives, through Jesus Christ our Lord. Amen. [From *Human Sexuality: A Christian Perspective.* Episcopal Church, U.S.A. 1992]

SESSION ONE

OBJECTIVE:

To reflect on the Purpose of the Study and experience part of the General Synod which initiated it.

Time: 60 minutes (including two video presentations and the break)

Run video (5 minutes)

Ask for three volunteers to read aloud the preamble and the two passages.

Purpose of the Study

A Word from the Primate and the Session Introduction

A WORD FROM THE PRIMATE, p. 3

BREAK

10 minutes

Bible Study and Reflection

VOICE 1: PREAMBLE

God reigns where there are people together who normally are not found together. These two passages are examples of divided people being united by Jesus Christ.

Scholars agree that the Letter to the Galatians is concerned with the question of whether Gentiles must become Jews before they can become Christians. Paul believes that a person becomes right with God only by faith in Jesus Christ. Our text is the central part of the letter which is an exposition of the doctrine of justification by faith alone (Galatians 3:1-4:31). The last part of the letter expresses concern about the abuse of Christian freedom.

The Letter to the Ephesians celebrates the union of the church with God through Jesus Christ and in the power of the Holy Spirit. The church is part of God's eternal purpose and included in the purpose is the ministry of reconciliation. Specifically this passage is about the reconciliation between Jew and non-Jew. The text can be expanded to include any groups which are divided. Reconciliation happens through Christ who has made both groups into one and who has broken down dividing walls. In Christ hostility can be turned into healing.

| SESSION ONE | 25 |

VOICE 2: GALATIANS 3:26-28

²⁶For in Christ Jesus you are all children of God through faith. ²⁷As many of you as were baptized into Christ have clothed yourselves with Christ. ²⁸There is no longer Jew or Greek, there is no longer slave or free, there is no longer male and female; for all of you are one in Christ Jesus.

VOICE 3: EPHESIANS 2:13-22

¹³Now in Christ Jesus you who once were far off have been brought near by the blood of Christ. ¹⁴For he is our peace; in his flesh he has made both groups into one and has broken down the dividing wall, that is, the hostility between us. ¹⁵He has abolished the law with its commandments and ordinances, that he might create in himself one new humanity in place of the two, thus making peace, ¹⁶and might reconcile both groups to God in one body through the cross, thus putting to death that hostility through it. ¹⁷So he came and proclaimed peace to you who were far off and peace to those who were near, ¹⁸for through him both of us have access in one Spirit to the Father. ¹⁹So then you are no longer strangers and aliens, but you are citizens with the saints and also members of the household of God, ²⁰built upon the foundation of the apostles and prophets, with Christ Jesus himself as the cornerstone. ²¹In him the whole structure is joined together and grows into a holy temple in the Lord; ²²in whom you also are built together spiritually into a dwelling place for God.

Ask the participants to form small groups

Thinking about the Primate's message, p. 3, the **Purpose of the Study**, p. 6, and the Bible readings, discuss:

What do these passages reveal to us about our community, our relationship with God, and our relationship with each other?

or

How do these passages relate to the subject of this study? Which are the most important verses for you?

In the whole group:

Run the video. (30 minutes)

VIEWS ON SEXUAL ORIENTATION: GENERAL SYNOD 1992

At the conclusion of the video:

Write down three words or short phrases to describe how you are feeling right now, then share these with one other member of the group.

Time: 5 minutes

You may wish to prepare for closing by asking the group to stand, gathering into a circle, lighting a candle, observing a few moments of silence.

Closing Worship

Prayer

(say together)

God of peace,
your love is generous,
and reaches out to hold us in your embrace.
Fill our hearts with tenderness
for those to whom we are linked today.
Give us sympathy with each other's trials;
give us patience with each other's faults;
that we may grow in the likeness of Jesus
and share in the joy of your kingdom. *Amen.*

[From *A New Zealand Prayer Book*]

Where to go from here:

For further reading:

Boswell, J. **Christianity, Social Tolerance, and Homosexuality: Gay People in Western Europe from the Beginning of the Christian Era to the Fourteenth Century.** 1980. Chicago: University of Chicago Press.

Boswell, J. **Same Sex Unions in Premodern Europe.** 1994. New York: Villard Books.

Pellegrin, V. B. H. **To Live According to our Nature.** 1993. Nova Scotia: The Diocesan Book Room.

Pritchard, R.W. (Ed). **A Wholesome Example: Sexual Morality and the Episcopal Church.** 1993. Lexington: Bristol.

Reed, J. (Ed.). **A Study Resource on Human Sexuality: Approaches to Sexuality and Christian Theology.** 1985. Toronto: Anglican Book Centre.

Reading for next session

A Christian Context for Sexuality & Intimacy by Diane Marshall, p. 28.

What Science is Saying by Dr. Donald Meen, p. 30.

For a more thorough discussion, a longer paper by Dr. Donald Meen, **The Contribution of Science to Understanding Homosexuality** is available from the Resource Centre, 600 Jarvis St., Toronto M4Y 2J6, or your diocesan office.

SESSION ONE 27

NOTES AND REFLECTIONS

At the end of each session, we leave you a sheet to jot down any ideas, thoughts, learnings from the session. These notes may help you in the task, at the end of this study, of formulating a message to our Church.

Please read before the next session

A Christian Context for Sexuality and Intimacy by Diane Marshall

Sexuality is fundamental to our very humanness, and in so many respects its expression relates to the profound human need for community. "It is not good that the human should be alone," records the Genesis narrative, and so God created another human – called male and female – in the goodness of the garden to become "one flesh," and based on a partnership of mutual self-giving love. Together, Adam and Eve were called into special relationship with God, to be stewards of the creation, and to be in relationship with one another as equal and interdependent persons. In the brokenness of the Fall, shame and domination usurped love and mutuality. But God has written love on our hearts, and Christ's life, death and resurrection have made possible the making of new relationships (Colossians 1) to which we are called to bear witness in the community of the Church.

The life of Jesus challenges us all, married and unmarried, to a more than genital love, a larger than biological family, a fruitfulness that goes beyond biological fecundity. Indeed, some of us build lives of deep intimacy that do not include genital sharing... . However in the midst of the challenges and invitations that surround our sexual lives, we proclaim our basic conviction: **sex is good.** (Whitehead and Whitehead, 1989)

Sex is also mysterious, and painful, and can be a source of profound alienation and confusion. "In sexual encounter we sometimes experience a communion so profound that it shatters the illusions of our isolation. We can also use sex to punish ourselves, and to control other people, to diminish joy." (Whitehead and Whitehead)

For Christians, sex is sacramental, reflecting the covenant of faithfulness and affection that God has made with us. As such, it does not exist in isolation, but is designed to be part of a covenant relationship which "protects and purifies the promises of sexual love." (Whitehead and Whitehead)

The desire for emotional intimacy — to know and be known — creates some of the most difficult human problems, because this desire is so easily confused with, and feels so much like, the desire for genital sexual union. Certainly intimacy and sexuality are closely allied; our desire for communion/union is one drive. But sexuality is not reducible to its genital expression. Everyone knows from human experience that we can have "sex" without intimacy, and intimacy without "sex".

A Christian psychiatrist, Gerald May, in his book *Will and Spirit* (1982) develops the thesis that the sexual desire and the unitive desire (the religious impulse) in human beings are the same. He says: " ... sexual and spiritual phenomena do seem to originate from the common energy source of all experience — the basic life force that we have chosen to call spirit ... . In its most fundamental sense, sexuality refers to basic life energy that is directed, differentiated, or transmitted into creative expressions or manifestations ... . The term 'genital' also reflects this creative quality of sexuality. In both Greek and Latin, the root 'gen', referring to being born or becoming, is the core of such words as 'genesis', 'genitive', and even 'generosity'.

In its fullest sense, then, sexuality is nothing other than creative spirit: basic energy directed towards the enrichment and expression of life. Further, it underscores the fact that an integration of sexuality is a fundamental concomitant of spiritual growth."

In other words, sexuality and spirituality are so intimately associated with what it means to be human that it is also possible that they can become confused with each other. Genital experience alone has little to do with the integration of full sexuality, and May goes on to say that "many very sexual, passionate, creative, spiritually mature people are celibate." Likewise, many "genitally active people are painfully uncrea-tive." A misdirection of sexual energy underlies many of the explosive and abusive areas of brokenness in gender relations today. Living in a sexually anxious age, our insecurities tend to centre around our body-image, sexual capabilities, social interest, and a fear of aloneness.

A theologian, James Nelson, has written extensively about our bodily selves. In his book *Embodiment*, (1978) he develops four interwoven themes in exploring the significance of the sexual body to Christian theology: feeling, desire, communion, and incarnation.

1) The *feeling* response to reality involves both cognition and emotion. It is the willingness to respond.. with as much of the totality of the self as one is able. It is the capacity to be deeply aroused by what we are experiencing. The term "body-self" describes the unity of the person. It is the refusal to be split into mind over body or heart over head, or to locate true selfhood in only part of the self.

2) The ancient Hebrews used the verb "to know" (yadah) as a synonym for sexual intercourse. The sexual act at its best is the union of *desiring* and knowing, in which the partner is treated as a self, "the treasured participant in communion".

3) "In its deepest experience sexuality is the desire for, and the expression of, *communion* of the self with other bodyselves and with God." It is an experience of unity, but not unification, since communion with another does not mean absorption. Thus, in sexual intercourse, it is a matter of "participation" rather than "possession."

4) Christian faith is an *incarnational* faith. "God is uniquely known to us through human presence, and human presence is always embodied presence."

The Evil One knows that the place to attack us is in an area where we are most subject to shame: our bodiliness. But Jesus freely became body, and "body" is the metaphor for the Church (the "body of Christ"). Thus our sexuality, as all of life, must be "made new" by the transforming and reforming person of Christ to be part of committed, faithful, self-giving love which serves, and is blessed by, God. Whether we are celibate, or in covenant relationships, sexuality leads us to deep intimacy in the context of community.

"God's way of loving is the only licensed teacher of human sexuality. God's passion created ours. Our deep desiring is a relentless returning to that place where all things are one. We will learn to be properly sexual as we understand the properly passionate relationship that God has with us. And we will learn how to be properly spiritual as we come to understand the true character of human longing and affection." (Rohr, 1982)

Human beings are able to live without genital contact, but are not able to live without love, affection, touch, and communication. Thus the sexual desire pushes us towards relationship, and the desire for deep *connection*.

An Episcopalian priest, Norman Pittenger, in *Time to Consent*, describes six characteristics of a truly loving relationship:

1 commitment (free self-giving to each other)
2 mutuality (in giving and receiving)
3 tenderness (versus coercion or cruelty)
4 hopefulness (each serving the other's growth into maturity)
5 faithfulness (intention of lifelong relationship)
6 desire for union

Our media saturated age often portrays sex as a demeaning and out-of-control passion, with little connection to intimacy or spirituality. Sexuality that dehumanizes or assaults another, or which is predatory, promiscuous or voyeuristic, is a violation of God's creation and gift of faithful and committed intimate communion with another person, made in God's image. (Gen.1:27)

Ms. Diane Marshall, a family therapist in Toronto is a member of the Task Force on Homosexuality and Homosexual Relationships.

What Science is Saying by Dr. Donald Meen

Please read before the next session

What does science have to offer us in our understanding of homosexuality?
Many people now look to science for answers to important questions about homosexuality. Science has contributed a great deal to our understanding, and while much is now known, much is also in the process of becoming known. Scientific knowledge develops incrementally: we keep building on and modifying our understanding so it better, and better captures "real life".

Particularly valuable to us is that science offers a *systematic* method of observing, developing theories about what we observe, *and testing out those theories*. Homosexuality is a topic about which theories abound! These can be evaluated rigorously by a careful, scientific examination of the evidence. Indeed, many conclusions, opinions and theories have been shown not to square with the facts. Others have fared better, and this incremental process of building scientific knowledge about homosexuality continues.

How do we know a scientific study is a good one?
It is true that not all studies presented as "scientific" are of the same quality. This has a lot to do with how carefully the study was designed and conducted. It is especially important that there be good controls against any effects of bias. In the end, results are considered valid if *independent* researchers, doing exactly what the original scientist did, find the same results.

Also, what the researcher is entitled to conclude from a study depends on the design of the study in the first place. Almost all the research in the area of homosexuality is what is termed "descriptive" research. It describes what the people in the scientist's sample are like. It can tell us what things *are like* for them, but it cannot tell us that something *caused* something else to happen in them. And, while it can tell us what things are like in *this sample of people,* it may not allow us to generalize to what things are like for other people. It all depends on how *representative* our sample is of some larger group of people we want to know about. This is a particular problem in research on homosexuality. Since homo-sexually-oriented people are an "invisible minority", it is virtually impossible to find a sample that we know is representative. Conclusions about "typical" characteristics of homosexually-oriented people are therefore always highly suspect.

What is sexual orientation, and specifically, homosexual orientation?
Probably the definition which encompasses most of the qualities of our sexual orientation is this: it is our potential to "fall in love with" someone of the other sex (heterosexual), the same sex (homosexual), or either sex (bisexual). It is our inner feeling of romantic, erotic attraction, whether or not we act on it.

How does this relate to whether a person sees himself or herself as a man or woman, and whether people behave the way most men or women do?
Sexual orientation is just one aspect of our sexual identity, and shouldn't be confused with the others: "gender identity" ("I am male. I am female."), "social sex role behaviour" (cultural images of what a man or woman "behaves like"), or biological sex. The vast majority of gay men who have been studied see themselves as men; while the vast majority of lesbian women see themselves as women. While there are "effeminate" gay men and "masculine" lesbians, studies suggest that most are indistinguishable from other people of the same sex. There are, of course, "effeminate" heterosexual men and "masculine" heterosexual women, too, just to complicate the picture, and cultural ideals of manliness and womanliness do change across societies and over time.

Just how many homosexually-oriented people are we talking about anyway?
Studies consistently show that a small minority of people have an exclusive or predominant homosexual orientation over their lives. An additional small minority report bisexual orientation. A larger proportion of people have at some time in their lives had at least some homosexual attraction or experience. Homosexual orientation appears to be twice as common among men as among women. A majority of people report exclusively heterosexual orientation.

The most recent large scale and representative sample of Americans studied (Janus and Janus, 1993) puts the numbers at 9% of men and 5% of women having frequent or ongoing homosexual experiences, with 4% of men and 2% of women describing themselves as homosexual, 5% of men and 3% of women as bisexual. Though 22% of men and 17% of women had homosexual experiences, 91% of men and 95% of women nonetheless described themselves as heterosexual.

This doesn't look like an "either or" situation.
Right. Beginning in the 1940's, systematic research has consistently

shown that sexual orientation is best thought of as being along a continuum. While some people are exclusively homosexual or heterosexual over their lives, others describe varying degrees of bisexual attraction, from the incidental to the significant.

What about the families of gay/lesbian people?

Well, first of all, though there have been any number of claims made about gay/lesbian people's families-of-origin, systematic study has shown no family characteristic which appears only in their families, and never in the families of heterosexual people. And differences, when they have been found, are only in degree. There is no solid evidence that gay/lesbian people's families-of-origin are necessarily any more, or less, dysfunctional than those of heterosexual people.

And we should be aware that there is more to one's family than family-of-origin. Gay/lesbian people also create their own families. A substantial minority are at some time in their lives in heterosexual marriages, and up to half of those who marry have children. (Significant differences in overall parenting effectiveness between gay/lesbian and heterosexual parents has not been shown.)

Furthermore, about half or more of people in large samples studied are found to be in primary intimate relationships — couples. There is plenty of evidence that these couples can be as functional as heterosexual couples can, and that their relationships develop along similar lines. It does appear that more gay male couples choose to have relationships which are not sexually exclusive ("monogamous") than lesbian or heterosexual couples do.

For gay/lesbian people, families "of choice" often include a network of close friends.

When you add it all up, a significant proportion of Canadians could have a very personal, family connection with a lesbian woman or gay man.

How do parents of lesbian/gay people react when they find out about their children's sexual orientation?

The research doesn't show only one pattern of response. For some parents, there are stages of dealing with it, from having their suspicions, through the impact of finding out for sure, to adjustment, resolution and family re-integration around the new reality. Some parents initially see their child as a stranger. Some feel guilty that they have "failed", or are angry or disgusted. For some, there is a struggle between their desire to love and accept, and their desire to be acceptable and respectable to others. Many are afraid or sad for their children, and report going through a process of grieving, moving from shock through to acceptance.

What is it like for homosexually-oriented youth?

Surveys show that young people may still be somewhat unsure of their orientation. They may feel alienated from peers and family by their "secret", and struggle with the negative stereotypes and hostility toward lesbian/gay people which they hear expressed around them.

Good relationships with their parents appear to be related to how comfortable and accepting of their orientation these young people are, how satisfactory their self-esteem, and how likely they are to "come out" to their parents.

What causes homosexuality?

At this point we cannot answer definitively what causes sexual orientation of any kind. Researchers have considered characteristics of lesbian/gay people's early social environment. There has yet to be substantiated any factor of family or peer relationships, early sexual experience, gender conformity, or any combination of these which distinguishes homosexual from heterosexual people in all cases. In short, we do not know what environmental factors may exert causal influence on sexual orientation, and the research, being entirely descriptive in design, cannot tell us.

There has been considerable recent interest in innate factors — the influence of genes and hormones. As yet unreplicated studies have identified differences in brain structures and some genetic material between heterosexual and homosexual people. Studies of twins consistently show that there is a much greater likelihood of finding that if one identical twin is lesbian or gay, the other is. This is less likely between non-identical twins, and less likely again between non-twin brothers or sisters. However, at this time, solid scientific evidence of what innate, biological factors causally influence sexual orientation is not in hand.

More and more scientists look to a model where innate and biological factors interact with learned and social environment factors to influence sexual orientation.

Can sexual orientation change?

As we have seen, some people report variability in their orientations over their lifetimes, while most report that their orientations have been quite consistently heterosexual or homosexual.

Bisexual people may look as if they change orientation, but we could also consider them to be expressing one or the other aspect of their bisexual orientation.

There has been considerable interest in "re-orienting" lesbian/gay people toward heterosexuality. Research in the area is particularly poorly done, but a pattern seems to emerge that for some people, usually those more bisexual than homosexual, some changes of uncertain duration, and more in behaviour than feelings, may follow some "treatments".

However, there is no scientific substantiation that "re-orientation" therapies of any sort change the sexual orientation of lesbian/gay people.

Is homosexuality some kind of mental disorder?

The predominant view among mental health professionals in the past, shared by some even today, was that homosexuality was pathological. In North America this is no longer the predominant view of professionals, since research has consistently identified "healthy homosexuals" — that is, lesbian and gay people who show no evidence of having any more psychological or social problems than heterosexual people. Being different from most people has not been found to mean being less psychologically healthy.

One particularly disturbing accusation is made by some that gay/lesbian people are prone to child sexual molestation. Systematic research shows that little of this involves homosexually-oriented people, the vast bulk of offences being by males against girls.

Aren't there special pressures on lesbian/gay people?

In fact, given a social climate which can still be hostile and rejecting, lesbian/gay people must continually deal with being stigmatized. There continues to be anti-gay violence and discrimination, which attacks from the outside. Since lesbian/gay people grow up hearing mostly disapproving messages about people of their sexual orientation, they often internalize anti-gay attitudes, which can attack them from within. This is especially difficult for lesbian/gay youth, who are estimated to comprise as many as 30% of youth suicides.

What is "coming out"?

As lesbian/gay people come to value themselves as homosexually-oriented, they integrate their orientation in a positive way into their personal identity. This is the foundation of "coming out". Identity formation and coming out can be described as occurring in four stages (Troiden, 1993): 1. sensitization, which includes feeling "different" from childhood peers of the same sex; 2. identity confusion, when one is not sure, but considers that one "could be" homosexual; 3. identity assumption, when one tolerates, then accepts, oneself as lesbian or gay; 4. commitment, when one has integrated one's orientation into one's life, based on self-acceptance.

"Coming" out is first a recognition and acceptance of oneself as lesbian or gay, then sharing this aspect of oneself with others — other gay/lesbian people, close heterosexual friends, brothers and sisters, parents, work colleagues, and the wider public.

What is "the homosexual lifestyle"?

That is hard to say, since we have no way of knowing what is truly "typical" for lesbian and gay people. It would be more accurate to speak of lifestyles, and these are many and varied. The bulk of the lives of lesbian/gay people is occupied by the same things that occupy heterosexual people — making a living, looking after physical, emotional, social and spiritual needs, building and maintaining relationships, paying rent or mortgages, planning holidays or retirement, contributing to community and church, and so on. Some are in couples, some are "swinging singles", some have children, others do not. They cover the range of religious and political beliefs, professions, trades and occupations, and recreational pursuits. In the end, what really distinguishes all lesbian/gay from all heterosexual people is not lifestyle, but the sex of the person with whom they "fall in love".

Dr. Donald Meen, a clinical psychologist in Vancouver, is a member of the Task Force on Homosexuality and Homosexual Relationships.

For a more thorough discussion, a longer paper by Dr. Meen, **The Contribution of Science to Understanding Homosexuality** is available from the Resource Centre, 600 Jarvis St., Toronto M4Y 2J6, or your diocesan office.

SESSION TWO 33

2

Seeking Understanding –
Three Contexts of Experience: Spiritual, Interpersonal, and Scientific

OBJECTIVE:

To rebuild the group; welcome any newcomers; review Our Group Standards.

Time: 20 minutes.

SESSION GOALS

- To consider a Christian context for discussing homosexuality and homosexual relationships.
- To consider the characteristics of intimate Christian relationships.
- To hear from Canadian Anglican gay and lesbian people, and from a parent who affirms his son as gay, of their journeys to self-affirmation.
- To become acquainted with current scientific knowledge.

GATHERING: WELCOMING NEWCOMERS

REBUILDING THE GROUP AND WELCOMING NEWCOMERS

Begin by asking people to introduce themselves

IF THERE ARE NEWCOMERS:

As a way of rebuilding the learning community, integrating newcomers and giving them something of the flavour of the first session, suggest that those who were there share with the newcomers by finishing the sentence —

The most valuable thing for me about our first meeting was...

Ask the newcomers —

What are you hearing?

Or

What questions does this raise for you?

IF THERE ARE NO NEWCOMERS:

As a way of rebuilding the learning community, ask the participants to finish the sentence —

The most valuable thing for me about our first meeting was...

| SESSION TWO | 34 |

PRAYER

(say together)

Almighty God, who created us male and female and who calls us to share in the creative and reconciling power of your love; grant that through this study we may come to know your will for us as sexual creatures so that all we say and do may show forth the power of your love in our lives, through Jesus Christ our Lord. Amen. [from *Human Sexuality: A Christian Perspective* Province VII, Episcopal Church, U.S.A., 1992]

Or

A prayer from the Worship Resources, p. 87,

If this task was finished in Session 1, ask the participants to read the statement aloud together, or each take a turn reading one line each.

or

If this task was delegated for further work following Session 1, ask the working group to present the statement for comment, revision and agreement.

Run video (1 minute)

REVIEW OUR GROUP STANDARDS

THE SESSION INTRODUCTION

You may wish to acknowledge that a great deal of information will be dealt with during this session.

| SESSION TWO | 35 |

OBJECTIVE:

To reflect on a Christian context for discussing the issues of homosexuality and homosexual relationships.

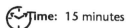 Time: 15 minutes

Ask the participants to form pairs.

A CHRISTIAN CONTEXT FOR SEXUALITY AND INTIMACY

Reflecting on the reading, *A Christian Context for Sexuality and Intimacy*, p. 28, discuss:

How did you feel after reading this article?

Think about the messages you have lived with about sex and your sexuality. How are these messages alike or different from the images in the reading?

OBJECTIVE:

To explore the relationship between life experience and a Christian definition of intimate relationships; to hear from some Canadian Anglican gay and lesbian people, and from a parent who affirms his son as gay, of their journeys to self-affirmation and acceptance.

 Time: 40 minutes.

Please read the following statement to the participants.

Run the video (15 minutes)

Ask participants to form small groups

If there is time, ask if there is anything anyone would like to share with the whole group.

VOICES — AN INTERPERSONAL CONTEXT AND JOURNEY TO SELF-AFFIRMATION

The stories on this video segment are those of persons whose struggle has led them to affirm themselves as lesbian or gay. Also included is a story of a parent who affirms his son as gay. To reflect the diversity of gay and lesbian experience within our church, a fuller range of voices will be heard in Session 5, Living Out Our Baptismal Covenants.

Discuss,

What ideas, images or words are most striking to you? Why?

BREAK

10 minutes

| SESSION TWO | 36 |

OBJECTIVE:

To present up-to-date information on psychosocial and biomedical research.

 Time: 30 minutes

Ask the participants to form pairs.

The task of the pairs is to hear each other. Questions may be asked for clarification only.

In the whole group

Recognizing that this session has dealt with a great deal of information, ask the participants...

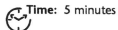**Time:** 5 minutes

Come together in a circle.

You may wish to light a candle and/or observe a few minutes of silence.

WHAT SCIENCE IS SAYING

Considering the paper *What Science is Saying,* p. 30, discuss:

What new information has been brought to your attention? Can you relate the information and opinions discussed in this article with your own beliefs and understandings about homosexuality and homosexual relationships?

What are you finding easy to hear and read about this issue? What makes sense to you? Why do you think this is the case?

What are you finding difficult to hear and read about this issue? Why?

Discuss,

Is there anything from your conversations you would like to share with the whole group?

How can we relate the opinions of science to what we believe about homosexuality and homosexual relationships?

What do you need to do in order for this information to be useful to you? (For example, have more time to reflect; continue the conversation with someone through the week, do more reading....)

CLOSING WORSHIP

Read Matthew 5:1-12 aloud — one person reading a verse each, going around the group.

SESSION TWO

Matthew 5:1-12

¹ When Jesus saw the crowds, he went up the mountain; and after he sat down, his disciples came to him.
² Then he began to speak, and taught them, saying:
³ Blessed are the poor in spirit, for theirs is the kingdom of heaven.
⁴ Blessed are those who mourn, for they will be comforted.
⁵ Blessed are the meek, for they will inherit the earth.
⁶ Blessed are those who hunger and thirst for righteousness, for they will be filled.
⁷ Blessed are the merciful, for they will receive mercy.
⁸ Blessed are the pure in heart, for they will see God.
⁹ Blessed are the peacemakers, for they will be called children of God.
¹⁰ Blessed are those who are persecuted for righteousness' sake, for theirs is the kingdom of heaven.
¹¹ Blessed are you when people revile you and persecute you and utter all kinds of evil against you falsely on my account.
¹² Rejoice and be glad, for your reward is great in heaven, for in the same way they persecuted the prophets who were before you.

PRAYER

Say together a closing prayer.

Choose a closing prayer from the Worship Resources, p. 87.

WHERE TO GO FROM HERE:

FOR FURTHER READING

Burr, C. *"Homosexuality and Biology,"* **The Atlantic Monthly**, 271(3), 1993, pp. 47-65.

Garnets, L.D. and Kimel, D.C. **Social Science: Psychological Perspectives on Lesbian and Gay Male Experience.** 1993. New York. Columbia University Press.

Gonsiorek, J.C. and Weinrich, J.D. (Eds.) **Homosexuality; Research Implications for Public Policy.** 1991. Newbury Park. Sage Publications.

May, G. **Will and Spirit.** 1982. San Francisco: Harper and Row.

Nelson, J.B. **Embodiment: An Approach to Sexuality and Christian Theology.** 1978. Minneapolis: Augsburg Press.

Nelson, J. **Between Two Gardens: Reflections on Sexuality and Religious Experience.** 1983. New York: Pilgrim Press.

Peck, M.S. **The Road Less Traveled: A New Psychology of Love, Traditional Values, and Spiritual Growth.** 1978. New York: Simon and Schuster.

Pittenger, W.N. **Time For Consent: A Christian's Approach to Homosexuality.** 1976. London: SCM.

Rohr, R. *"The holiness of human sexuality,"* Sojourners. October, 1982.

Spong, J.S. **Living in Sin?: A Bishop Rethinks Human Sexuality.** 1988. San Francisco: Harper and Row.

Whitehead, E.E. and Whitehead, J.D. **A Sense of Sexuality: Christian Love and Intimacy.** 1989. New York: Doubleday.

RESOURCES FOR FAMILIES

Parents — FLAG, About our Children. 1012 14 St. N.W. Ste. 700 Washington, D.C. 20005

Fairchild, B. and Hayward, **Now That You Know: What Every Parent Should Know about Homosexuality.** 1979. New York: Harcourt Brace Jovanovich.

Clark, D. **Loving Someone Gay.** 1987. Berkeley, CA: Celestial Arts.

Borhek, M.V. **Coming Out to Parents. A Two-Way Survival Guide for Lesbians and Gay Men and their Parents.** 1983. New York: Pilgrim.

READING FOR THE NEXT SESSION

Sexual Orientation and the New Testament by Dr. Terence L. Donaldson, p. 40.

Reading Some Biblical Passages Often Associated with Homosexuality and Homosexual Relationships by the Rev. Dr. George Porter., p. 42.

SESSION TWO 39

NOTES AND REFLECTIONS

Please read before the next session

Sexual Orientation and the New Testament

by Dr. Terence Donaldson

Note: This reading is a condensation of the video presentation you will see in Session 3.

Introduction

Thank you for the invitation to play a part in an important issue within the church, which needs to be discussed seriously, openly and thoroughly.

My goal here is not to argue a case, or to defend a position, but to lay before you some of the factors to be considered in discerning both what the biblical texts meant in their original contexts, and what they might mean for us today. In fairness, though, I should say something about where I am coming from on the issue. The best description is the "uneasy middle". I feel torn between two realities, and two commitments.

On the one hand, there is my upbringing in the church, which has given me a positive appreciation of the Bible, and a strong identification with orthodox Christian tradition. Tradition has understood heterosexual marriage to be the normative context for the physical expression of human sexuality.

On the other hand, there is the actual experience of real people, some of them friends and colleagues, equally committed to Christ and church, who experience same-sex orientation as a given part of who they are, and same-sex relationships as nurturing and grace-filled.

Again, on the one hand, I can appreciate the anxiety of many in the church, who fear that the centre of the faith will not be able to hold, if experience is elevated to the level of revelation, and is allowed to function as our primary authority, overriding scripture and tradition.

Yet on the other hand, I am well aware that Christian life is a pilgrimage, and that in a whole range of issues (slavery, the ministry of women, divorce) we in the church have entered new territory, unforeseen in the Bible, without losing our basic sense of direction.

And so I find myself in the uneasy middle, tugged by compelling forces in both directions. In some ways, I think things are easier at the extremes. If I believed that every sentence in the Bible was the direct word of God to us, so that every declarative sentence in scripture represented God's will and command, or if, at the other extreme, I believed that God is primarily encountered in subjective personal experience, that what is experienced as a given must therefore of necessity be a gift, and that the Bible is at best an interesting relic from the past, and at worst an unredeemable instrument of oppression, if I found myself at either of these extreme positions, then I wouldn't be faced with the same internal struggle. But I find both of these extremes unpalatable, and so, I suspect, do many in the Anglican church.

And so I find myself in the middle, not simply because the forces tugging me in opposite directions cancel each other out, but because this is where I feel I need to be. I deplore the kind of polarization that tends to take place over this issue, with strident ideologies of left and right forcing those in between to run for cover. I think that the way we carry out the debate will be as important in the long run as the position we arrive at.

So I would like to find ways to turn the uneasy middle into the creative and faithful middle. The Bible is appealed to in different ways by all participants in the discussion. Consequently, the process of interpreting what the Bible has to say on the issue is one in which interpreters feel pulled in different directions — in one way by voices speaking more from tradition, in another way by voices speaking more on the basis of experience.

What I want to do is to give a sense of these "to and fro" pulls as they emerge in the interpretation of one of the key passages. Some of these pulls have to do with the question of what the text meant in its original context; others have to do with the matter of how the text is to be interpreted for our own context. The result will be a kind of catalogue of factors to be taken into account in any discussion. I will conclude with some general observations about the process of interpretation.

The Text – Romans 1: 26-27

Just a handful of biblical texts touch on the issue of same-sex relations. For various reasons, I will concentrate on Romans 1:26-27. I choose Romans because here is the only place where we have a more extended theological discussion. Also, it is the only place where both sexes are mentioned.

Rom. 1:26-27

[26]For this reason God gave them up to degrading passions. Their women exchanged natural intercourse for unnatural, [27]and in the same way also the men, giving up natural intercourse with women, were consumed with passion for one another. Men committed shameless acts with men and received in their own persons the due penalty for their error.

The Discussion

Voices from Tradition:
The Plain Sense
The plain sense of the text is a clear statement that sexual intercourse between members of the same sex is contrary to God's will and purposes.

Voices from Experience:
The Homiletical Sting Operation
What Paul is doing in the passage is not condemning same-sex activity as such, but cleverly capitalizing on the overeagerness of his opponents in the debate to condemn others, including others involved in same-sex relations.

Voices from Tradition:
Jewish and Christian Consensus
Nevertheless, the consensus in the Old Testament, first century Judaism, and in the early church was one of opposition to homosexual practice, and Paul clearly shared that consensus.

Voices from Experience:
Greco-Roman Practice
But the only form of homosexual practice that Paul would have been aware of was pederasty — i.e. unequal relations between an adult male and an adolescent boy. Consequently, his statements have no bearing on the present issue.

Voices from Tradition:
Heterosexual Marriage as the Biblical Norm
Paul's statements are not based simply on a *negative* opinion of same-sex acts (as these existed in his own culture), but more fundamentally on the *positive* conviction that heterosexual marriage is the divinely intended norm for sexual expression.

Voices from Experience:
Givenness of Sexual Orientation
But the most crucial factor in the discussion is this: the widespread witness from gays and lesbians that their attraction to persons of the same sex is a given and unchangeable part of their personal makeup — something they didn't choose; something that they have tried to change, often appealing to God for help; something that they have had to accept as part of who they are.

Voices from Tradition:
"Givenness" and Paul's View of Sin
But "givenness" is precisely Paul's point in Romans 1. Because humankind has fundamentally rejected God, God has "given them up" to various patterns of behaviour — patterns that come with the territory for a race that has abandoned God; patterns, in other words, that are "given" rather than freely chosen.

Voices from Experience:
"Givenness" Once More
Still, same-sex orientation is a reality that needs to be addressed. On a whole variety of issues - from the inclusion of the Gentiles in New Testament times, through slavery, the role of women, and the reality of divorce — the church has been led to decisions and positions that might run counter to the Bible at the surface level, but are in harmony with the spirit and direction of the Bible at a deeper level.

Concluding Reflections
Such are the voices that I hear as I read this passage in the context of the contemporary discussion. I do not try to play the role of adjudicator, prescribing which voices should be given precedence, or which arguments should be given more weight than others. This is a task for the church as a whole, under the guidance of the Holy Spirit.

For my part, I am still wrestling, wanting both to be faithful to the orthodox faith of church as we have received it, and to be open to the possibility that others have experienced God in different ways. Nevertheless, a few concluding observations.

As I consider the early church and its way of dealing with contentious issues, I identify the following points that I think can serve as touchstones and guidelines:

1. Common commitment to the gospel as a starting point for discussion.
2. A church conscious of its call to be a distinctive counter-culture, as the context for discussion.
3. A recognition that the Christian way is a path of discipleship, one that makes demands on all of us, and will cut across most of our natural inclinations and tendencies.
4. A willingness to take seriously and grant an empathetic hearing to all who share this starting point, context and path.
5. A willingness to re-examine tradition, from the starting point of the gospel, in the light of new experiences.
6. A concern to find faithful and creative resolutions that will preserve the unity and mission of the church.

*Dr. Terence L. Donaldson
teaches at the
College of Emmanuel & St. Chad
in Saskatoon, Saskatchewan.*

Reading Some Biblical Passages Often Associated with Homosexuality and Homosexual Relationships

by The Rev. Dr. George Porter

The biblical passages referred to in this article are found at the end, pp 44-46.
As the church undertakes the study of homosexuality and homosexual relationships, a variety of voices can be heard speaking about the many issues involved. When Anglicans approach the biblical material believed to be relevant, these voices can be heard echoing several divergent perspectives.

Within these discussions are a number of specific texts to which reference is commonly made. These include:
Genesis 19:1-11
Leviticus 20: 7-22
Ruth 1:6-18
1 Timothy 1:8-11
1 Corinthians 6:9-11
2 Samuel 1:5-12, 17-27.

More recently, the creation accounts of Genesis 1 and 2, passages referring to marriage, and the stories of Ruth/Naomi and Jonathan/David relationships have been considered.

As these passages come into the discussion, one must keep in mind a fundamental principle of biblical interpretation: Texts without contexts become pretexts.

In other words, biblical material must be understood in light of the environment in which it occurs. Passages have historical, cultural, linguistic and literary contexts. They cannot be properly understood apart from these settings, and, if not properly understood, will not be of much value in informing the mind of the church today in the particular contexts in which it seeks to live the life of the people of God.

Genesis 19:1-11 (usually taken along with the parallel Judges 19:14-20:11 passage) has long been associated in the minds of most Canadians with homosexuality. Depicting what is generally understood to be an attempted sexual assault on two male guests at the home of Lot in Sodom, it has given rise to the English use of the term 'sodomy' in reference to male homosexual intercourse. This association remains quite strong in the minds of many Anglicans.

Other understandings have been voiced, however. One notes that the Hebrew word translated 'know' does not necessarily have sexual associations and, even when it does, it does not appear in homosexual contexts. Therefore, in this view, the story does not involve sex at all. Instead, it has to do only with violations of the hospitality codes of that era — something for which Sodom is repeatedly noted in other references in the Hebrew scriptures.

Others identify sexual implications in the immediate context of the story, but argue that the nature of the sexual assault was part of this violation of hospitality codes. In the patriarchal context, where women were not highly valued as persons, for a man to be treated liked a woman was considered degrading. Homosexual assault was, therefore, not intended primarily as a sexual expression, but as deliberate humiliation. This says nothing about homosexual orientation.

Still others, recognizing the same sexual implications in the context of the passage, insist that it portrays only homosexual assault. As such, it really cannot be applied to consenting, committed relationships of love. Would changing the sex of the visitors, for example, imply that heterosexual assault (as occurred in the Gibeah incident) negate all heterosexual intercourse or relationships?

No similar violent implications appear in the Levitical passages. They seem quite clear in their prohibition of male-to-male intercourse, and in their prescription of the death penalty for those involved. Those who speak from this perspective observe that it is called 'an abomination', classifying all such intercourse as offensive to God and sinful, regardless of the circumstances in which it occurs.

Other voices note that many of the additional regulations, including the immediate context, are no longer regarded as binding. 'Why,' they ask, 'are these separated out for special regard?' If some are disregarded, should not all be disregarded?

In a similar way, some have argued that these regulations have only to do with ritual purity. Since intercourse involves semen, it would cause ritual, not moral, impurity. Such ritual laws are not followed today.

Another possibility, some argue, is that the offence is the non-productive use of semen. In a society struggling for survival and domination, births would be precious. Like Onan's 'spilling his seed upon the ground,' sexual intercourse between males could not biologically produce children. This may explain why lesbianism was not mentioned.

Yet another possibility arises from noting the linguistic and literary context. 'Abomination' is a technical word in the Hebrew scriptures referring to anything associated with idolatry, for example. Furthermore, the immediate context of these Levitical regulations reflects concerns with the idolatrous religious practices of the surrounding nations. This perspective identifies the prohibition as forbidding participation in those religious rites, rather than as a blanket condemnation of all homosexual intercourse under any and all circumstances.

The relationships of Ruth/Naomi and Jonathan/David have been hailed as inspiring stories of deep friendship and commitment. The fact that they involve persons of the same gender has been understood as excluding a specifically sexual aspect. Certainly none is clear from the immediate context.

Some assert, however, that grounds exist for seeing in these passages biblical role-models for gay and lesbian relationships. The focus is on intimacy between persons of the same gender. While the Ruth/Naomi relationship involves certain generational questions, Jonathan and David were essentially chronological peers. The account of the parting of Jonathan and David — in which their love for one another is said to surpass even love for a woman — a word is used for 'embrace', which is linguistically related to the root of the Hebrew expression for 'orgasm'.

The passages from I Corinthians and I Timothy have caused much recent discussion. In most English translations they appear to present homosexual acts as causes for exclusion from the Kingdom of God, or as something from which Christian converts had been delivered. In this way, they have been understood both as warnings and sources of hope. As the former, they warn people that engaging in homosexual acts is sinful. As the latter, since the text says something to the effect that 'such were some of you', implying that repentance, forgiveness and change are possible for homosexual persons.

The accuracy of translations has, however, been questioned. Particularly three words are at issue: 'pornoi', 'malakoi' and 'arsenokoitai'. The first is generally regarded as referring to any sort of immoral behaviour. The second, which literally means 'soft ones', and the third, which literally means 'ones who lie with men', are less clear. They do not appear in any other New Testament context, nor do they appear in the oldest post-testament Christian writers' discussions about homosexuality.

Given the lack of clarity about the meaning of these words, the lack of agreement about interpretation of these passages is not surprising. Some dismiss them out of hand as having nothing at all to do with any homosexual acts. Others say that they likely do refer to unequal homosexual relationships between boys (or boy slaves) and the men who lie with them — perhaps in a prostitution context. Still others suggest that once again the context is concerned with the idolatry of the non-Christian religions. The activities that are portrayed negatively as sexual — perhaps even homosexual — are acts in the context of religious prostitution. Either way, homosexual acts in the context of consenting, committed and loving relationships are not addressed.

When the creation account(s) of Genesis of 1 and 2 enter the discussions, one approach notes that the first humans were in some way created male and female. Same gender couples are not envisioned by the creation account(s).

In the heterosexual relationship, many would argue the image of God is most clearly realized or reflected. Originally the human was both male and female. The oneness expressed in the union — especially in the sexual union ('the two shall become one flesh') — of the sexes reflects that longing for restored oneness in a way which same-gender relationships (including sexual relationships) cannot. Two opposite and complementary halves are required, not two of the same half.

Others contend that relationship, not gender, is the focus of the creation account(s). What is at issue is companionship and commitment, over against isolation (loneliness) and chaos. Same-gender couples offer a relational context comparable to heterosexual couples, when one considers the loving environment in which people can move toward human fulfilment. This, rather than gender complementarity, most clearly reflects the divine image.

Similar positions revolve around the biblical marriage texts. On the one hand, while it is recognized that a considerable variety of relational patterns are exhibited in the biblical texts under the general title of marriage, these relationships are always heterosexual. These writings do not offer approved examples of homosexual relationships — loving, consenting, and covenanted or otherwise — because, it is argued, such relationships have no place in the divine intentions for human beings.

On the other hand, relationship, not gender, is the primary focus of biblical concern. Ideals of mutuality, commitment, love and security are of primary importance. None of the biblical writers lived in a cultural or historical context in which homosexual relationships would have been as thoroughly understood as they are today. In this view, relationships of deep caring which result in personal growth and satisfaction for those involved eclipse gender considerations.

As Christians wrestle with issues surrounding homosexuality and homosexual relationships, they hear many voices echoing many understandings in relationship to these biblical texts. This can be both bewildering and challenging as the Anglican Church of Canada seeks to hear authentic voices in its considerations.

The Rev. Dr. George Porter, Diocese of Brandon, is a member of the Task Force on Homosexuality and Homosexual Relationships.

Reading for Session Three

Please read before next session

Bible Readings

GENESIS 19:1-11

¹ The two angels came to Sodom in the evening, and Lot was sitting in the gateway of Sodom. When Lot saw them, he rose to meet them, and bowed down with his face to the ground. ² He said, "Please, my lords, turn aside to your servant's house and spend the night, and wash your feet; then you can rise early and go on your way." They said, "No; we will spend the night in the square." ³ But he urged them strongly; so they turned aside to him and entered his house; and he made them a feast, and baked unleavened bread, and they ate. ⁴ But before they lay down, the men of the city, the men of Sodom, both young and old, all the people to the last man, surrounded the house; ⁵ and they called to Lot, "Where are the men who came to you tonight? Bring them out to us, so that we may know them." ⁶ Lot went out of the door to the men, shut the door after him, ⁷ and said, "I beg you, my brothers, do not act so wickedly. ⁸ Look, I have two daughters who have not known a man; let me bring them out to you, and do to them as you please; only do nothing to these men, for they have come under the shelter of my roof." ⁹ But they replied, "Stand back!" And they said, "This fellow came here as an alien, and he would play the judge! Now we will deal worse with you than with them." Then they pressed hard against the man Lot, and came near the door to break it down. ¹⁰ But the men inside reached out their hands and brought Lot into the house with them, and shut the door. ¹¹ And they struck with blindness the men who were at the door of the house, both small and great, so that they were unable to find the door.

LEV. 20:7-22

⁷ Consecrate yourselves therefore, and be holy; for I am the LORD your God. ⁸ Keep my statutes, and observe them; I am the LORD; I sanctify you. ⁹ All who curse father or mother shall be put to death; having cursed father or mother, their blood is upon them. ¹⁰ If a man commits adultery with the wife of his neighbor, both the adulterer and the adulteress shall be put to death. ¹¹ The man who lies with his father's wife has uncovered his father's nakedness; both of them shall be put to death; their blood is upon them. ¹² If a man lies with his daughter-in-law, both of them shall be put to death; they have committed perversion, their blood is upon them. ¹³ If a man lies with a male as with a woman, both of them have committed an abomination; they shall be put to death; their blood is upon them. ¹⁴ If a man takes a wife and her mother also, it is depravity; they shall be burned to death, both he and they, that there may be no depravity among you. ¹⁵ If a man has sexual relations with an animal, he shall be put to death; and you shall kill the animal. ¹⁶ If a woman approaches any animal and has sexual relations with it, you shall kill the woman and the animal; they shall be put to death, their blood is upon them. ¹⁷ If a man takes his sister, a daughter of his father or a daughter of his mother, and sees her nakedness, and she sees his nakedness, it is a disgrace, and they shall be cut off in the sight of their people; he has uncovered his sister's nakedness, he shall be subject to punishment. ¹⁸ If a man lies with a woman having her sickness and uncovers her nakedness, he has laid bare her flow and she has laid bare her flow of blood; both of them shall be cut off from their people. ¹⁹ You shall not uncover the nakedness of your mother's sister or of your father's sister, for that is to lay bare one's own flesh; they shall be subject to punishment. ²⁰ If a man lies with his uncle's wife, he has uncovered his uncle's nakedness; they shall be subject to punishment; they shall die childless. ²¹ If a man takes his brother's wife, it is impurity; he has uncovered his brother's nakedness; they shall be childless. ²² You shall keep all my statutes and all my ordinances, and observe them, so that the land to which I bring you to settle in may not vomit you out.

READING FOR SESSION THREE   45

RUTH 1:6-18

⁶ Then she started to return with her daughters-in-law from the country of Moab, for she had heard in the country of Moab that the Lord had considered his people and given them food. ⁷ So she set out from the place where she had been living, she and her two daughters-in-law, and they went on their way to go back to the land of Judah. ⁸ But Naomi said to her two daughters-in-law, "Go back each of you to your mother's house. May the Lord deal kindly with you, as you have dealt with the dead and with me. ⁹ The Lord grant that you may find security, each of you in the house of your husband." Then she kissed them, and they wept aloud. ¹⁰ They said to her, "No, we will return with you to your people." ¹¹ But Naomi said, "Turn back, my daughters, why will you go with me? Do I still have sons in my womb that they may become your husbands? ¹² Turn back, my daughters, go your way, for I am too old to have a husband. Even if I thought there was hope for me, even if I should have a husband tonight and bear sons, ¹³ would you then wait until they were grown? Would you then refrain from marring? No, my daughters, it has been far more bitter for me than for you, because the hand of the Lord has turned against me." ¹⁴ Then they wept aloud again. Orpah kissed her mother-in-law, but Ruth clung to her. ¹⁵ So she said, "See, you sister-in-law has gone back to her people and to her gods; return after your sister-in-law." ¹⁶ But Ruth said, "Do not press me to leave you or to turn back from following you! Where you go, I will go: Where you lodge, I will lodge; your people shall be my people, and your God my God. ¹⁷ Where you die, I will die — there will I be buried. May the Lord do thus and so to me, and more as well, if even death parts me from you!" ¹⁸ When Naomi saw that she was determined to go with her, she said no more to her.

1 TIMOTHY 1:8-11

⁸ Now we know that the law is good, if one uses it legitimately. ⁹ This means understanding that the law is laid down not for the innocent but for the lawless and disobedient, for the godless and sinful, for the unholy and profane, for those who kill their father or mother, for murderers, ¹⁰ fornicators, sodomites, slave traders, liars, perjurers, and whatever else is contrary to the sound teaching ¹¹ that conforms to the glorious gospel of the blessed God, which he entrusted to me.

1 CORINTHIANS 6:9-11

⁹ Do you not know that wrongdoers will not inherit the kingdom of God? Do not be deceived! Fornicators, idolaters, adulterers, male prostitutes, sodomites, ¹⁰ thieves, the greedy, drunkards, revilers, robbers— none of these will inherit the kingdom of God. ¹¹ And this is what some of you used to be. But you were washed, you were sanctified, you were justified in the name of the Lord Jesus Christ and in the Spirit of our God.

2 SAM. 1:5-12, 17-27

⁵ Then David asked the young man who was reporting to him, "How do you know that Saul and his son Jonathan died?" ⁶ The young man reporting to him said, "I happened to be on Mount Gilboa; and there was Saul leaning on his spear, while the chariots and the horsemen drew close to him. ⁷ When he looked behind him, he saw me, and called to me. I answered, `Here sir.' ⁸ And he said to me, `Who are you?' I answered him, `I am an Amalekite.' ⁹ He said to me, `Come, stand over me and kill me; for convulsions have seized me, and yet my life still lingers.' ¹⁰ So I stood over him, and killed him, for I knew that he could not live after he had fallen. I took the crown that was on his head and the armlet that was on his arm, and I have brought them here to my lord." ¹¹ Then David took hold of his clothes and tore them; and all the men who were with him did the same. ¹² They mourned and wept, and fasted until evening for Saul and for his son Jonathan, and for the army of the LORD and for the house of Israel, because they had fallen by the sword... ¹⁷ David intoned this lamentation over Saul and his son Jonathan. ¹⁸ (He ordered that The Song of the Bow be taught to the people of Judah; it is written in the Book of Jashar.) He said: ¹⁹ Your glory, O Israel, lies slain upon your high places! How the mighty have fallen! ²⁰ Tell it not in Gath, proclaim it not in the streets of Ashkelon; or the daughters of the Philistines will rejoice, the daughters of the uncircumcised will exult. ²¹ You mountains of Gilboa, let there be no dew or rain upon you, nor bounteous fields! For there the shield of the mighty was defiled, the shield of Saul, anointed with oil no more. ²² From the blood of the slain, from the fat of the mighty, the bow of Jonathan did not turn back, nor the sword of Saul return empty. ²³ Saul and Jonathan, beloved and lovely! In life and in death they were not divided; they were swifter than eagles, they were stronger than lions. ²⁴ O daughters of Israel, weep over Saul, who clothed you with crimson, in luxury, who put ornaments of gold on your apparel. ²⁵ How the mighty have fallen in the midst of the battle! Jonathan lies slain upon your high places. ²⁶ I am distressed for you, my brother Jonathan; greatly beloved were you to me; your love to me was wonderful, passing the love of women. ²⁷ How the mighty have fallen, and the weapons of war perished!

SESSION THREE 47

3

Seeking Understanding in the Bible

OBJECTIVE:

To rebuild the group and to review Our Group Standards

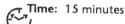Time: 15 minutes

SESSION GOALS

- To identify various ways the Bible is read and used.
- To hear diverse voices speak about how the biblical passages are applied to the issues of homosexuality and homosexual relationships.

GATHERING: REBUILDING THE GROUP

As a way of rebuilding the learning community ask the participants:

What, for you, were the highlights of the previous sessions?

Have you had any new insights since the last session?

PRAYER

Choose a prayer from the Worship Resources, p. 87.

Say together a prayer chosen from the Worship Resources

Ask the participants to read the statement aloud together or each take a turn reading one statement.

REVIEW OUR GROUP STANDARDS

Run video (2 minutes)

SESSION INTRODUCTION

At this and following sessions, use your discretion about how your group reviews its standards. See note in What we Learned in Testing the Program of Study, p.9.

SESSION THREE 48

OBJECTIVES:

To identify various ways the Bible is read and used; to hear and consider different understandings of biblical interpretation regarding homosexuality and homosexual relationships.

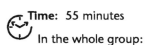
Time: 55 minutes

In the whole group:

Invite the participants to read aloud one sentence of the passage each, going around the group.

EXPLORING THE DIVERSITY

INTRODUCTION: READING THE TEXT

ROMANS 1:18-27

¹⁸For the wrath of God is revealed from heaven against all ungodliness and wickedness of those who by their wickedness suppress the truth.

¹⁹For what can be known about God is plain to them, because God has shown it to them.

²⁰Ever since the creation of the world his eternal power and divine nature, invisible though they are, have been understood and seen through the things he has made.

So they are without excuse; ²¹for though they knew God, they did not honour him as God or give thanks to him, but they became futile in their thinking, and their senseless minds were darkened.

²²Claiming to be wise, they became fools; ²³and they exchanged the glory of the immortal God for images resembling a mortal human being or birds or four-footed animals or reptiles.

²⁴Therefore God gave them up in the lusts of their hearts to impurity, to the degrading of their bodies among themselves, ²⁵because they exchanged the truth about God for a lie and worshipped and served the creature rather than the Creator, who is blessed forever! Amen.

²⁶For this reason God gave them up to degrading passions.

Their women exchanged natural intercourse for unnatural, ²⁷and in the same way also the men, giving up natural intercourse with women, were consumed with passion for one another.

Men committed shameless acts with men and received in their own persons the due penalty for their error.

Individual reflection:

What images and feelings does this passage evoke?

SESSION THREE 49

Run video (20 minutes)

ONE PERSON'S STRUGGLE — SEXUAL ORIENTATION AND THE NEW TESTAMENT

Ask participants to form small groups

Discuss:

What was new? Did you find any "Aha's!" in the various interpretations?

The task of the small groups is to hear each other. Ask questions for clarification only.

What makes the most sense to you? What fits with your own understanding? Why do you think this is the case?

What does not make sense to you? What makes you feel uncomfortable or confused? Why?

Do you have some questions? Are these questions new to you?

What are the guidelines and principles that you bring to interpreting the scriptures.

In the whole group, ask participants:

Is there anything you would like to tell the whole group about your small group conversations?

BREAK
10 minutes

OBJECTIVE:

To identify various ways the Bible is read and used. To participate in creating a "To and Fro" dialogue with each other.

THINKING ABOUT BIBLICAL INTERPRETATION

BIBLE STUDY: "TO AND FRO" WITH THE TEXT

In the video you have just seen, Dr. Terry Donaldson creates a "to and fro" conversation with the Romans I text in order to explore the different interpretative voices. Similarly, the Rev. Dr. George Porter explores some diverse ways of interpreting various other biblical passages in *Reading Some Biblical Passages Often Associated with Homosexuality and Homosexual Relationships*.

Time: 35 minutes

SESSION THREE   50

Ask the participants to form small groups

Participants may want to use the *Sexual Orientation and the New Testament* or *Reading Some Biblical Passages Often Associated with Homosexuality and Homosexual Relationships* papers as models to help their conversation get started.

Remind the participants that, while working together, the most helpful questions will be questions for clarification.

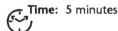
Time: 5 minutes

In the whole group:

You may wish to prepare for closing by gathering into a circle, lighting a candle, observing a few moments of silence.

You may want to write down on newsprint some of the reflections which emerge in the whole group conversation, noting the "Aha's!", questions, and even the diverse observations which have emerged during this session.

Choose a prayer from the Worship Resources, p. 87.

Choose one passage from the Bible readings found on pp 43-45 and create your own "To and Fro" conversation based on that text.

Closing Worship

Ask participants

Is there anything you would like to tell the whole group about your small group conversations?

What did you find most challenging from the discussions you have had? What are your "Aha's!"

What more do you need to know? How can you find this out [reading, research, more conversation...]?

Prayers

Say together a closing prayer.

Where to Go From Here

For further study

Countryman, L.W. **Dirt, Greed and Sin: Sexual Ethics in the New Testament and Their Implications for Today.** 1988. Philadelphia: Fortress.

McNeil, J.J. **Taking a Chance on God: Liberating Theology for Gays, Lesbians, and Their Lovers. Families and Friends.** 1988. Boston: Beacon Press.

Comstock, G. D. **Gay Theology Without Apology.** 1993. Cleveland: Pilgrim.

Pittinger, W. N. **Making Sexuality Human.** 1970. New York: Pilgrim.

Scroggs, R. **The New Testament and Homosexuality: Contextual Background for Contemporary Debate.** 1983. Philadelphia: Fortress.

Reading for the next session

Conversation About Ethics with the Rev. Tom Mabey, p. 53.

| SESSION THREE | 52 | . . . .

◀ NOTES AND REFLECTIONS

Please read before the next session

Conversation About Ethics with Tom Mabey

I know the word "ethics" refers to what is right and wrong, but can you explain how it works in practice?

We all live with many beliefs and assumptions about what is right and wrong, good and bad. We call these our *values*. They include convictions like, "human life is good and should be respected", "pain should not be inflicted on others", and more complex ones too. Our value commitments are often almost like unconscious baggage we carry, taking them for granted. We acquire them from fundamental experiences and from culture. They can be changed, but because they are our moral identity, changing them is a difficult, painful conversion process. When we make practical decisions about what we ought or ought not to do in particular situations in the light of these values we enter the world of *morality*. *Ethics* is the form of thinking we use to translate our values into moral judgements about our actions, and to ground our moral judgements in our values.

Well there must be as many ways of thinking as there are people. Does that mean there are as many kinds of ethics as there are people?

There are certainly different kinds of ethical thinking, but practically we can identify three major groupings. I will give a key word for each. One method we might call *duty ethics* and a second, *naturalist ethics*. The third is more difficult to describe, but I will call it *interactive ethics*. People using the duty method to evaluate actions tend to ask: 'Is this action right, is it in accordance with the rules?' Those using the natural method would ask 'Is this action good; does it fulfil rational ends and purposes?' People using the interactive method would ask 'Is this action responsible, does it respond appropriately and creatively to what is going on in this situation?'

Does this mean there are different standards, that there are differences between being right, or good or responsible?

Well, there are certainly different ways of reaching ethical conclusions. People who think in terms of duty are likely to think something is right or wrong because an authority has said so. Stealing is wrong because the Ten Commandments prohibit it. Moral people obey the code of behaviour expected by those who hold power and express it in laws and precepts. They value the kind of justice that maintains orderly life and punishes disorder.

And what about the naturalist method of ethical thinking?

People whose ethics are dominated by the naturalist method are likely to think according to a rational calculation of means and ends. They assume that the world is reasonably constructed according to a plan to achieve a purpose. Actions are good or bad because they fulfil (or frustrate) what nature appears to intend, or because they are useful (or not) in achieving human goals. If something has a purpose in the world, it is irrational and bad to frustrate that purpose; or if society determines that something is useful for achieving the happiness of human beings, it is irrational and bad to undermine that good. They might argue that if it is natural, or socially useful for children to be nurtured by two parents, it is wrong for people to choose intentionally to be single parents. They value the kind of contractual justice in which rational agreements freely arrived at provide the social fabric.

And the third ethical method?

The two methods of ethical thinking we have looked at view people basically as individuals connected primarily through law or reason. They determine what it is moral to do or not to do by applying their codes or their principles to decisions in actual situations. The third method regards people as being who they are because of their relationships. As moral agents they ask what behaviour will foster the development of mature human relationships. Which actions in a given set of conditions will be a creative, constructive response to the potential for healthy and whole relationships? Such behaviour they regard as responsible. They do not so much apply precepts and principles to the situation, as try to ask discerning questions about what will respond appropriately to the values at stake. This can lead the person who thinks interactively into conflict with conclusions drawn by those thinking in other ways. For example, the Bible says "What God has joined together, let no one put assunder". But many discerning people recognize that it is sometimes responsible for an abused woman to separate from a violent husband for her own sake and that of her children. They value a justice which calls persons to account for their actions in terms of their embodiment of relationships of solidarity.

Are you suggesting that the first two methods are outdated and that only the interactive method of ethical thinking should be used?

Not at all. In fact all three are used by all of us. But for most people one or other of the three will be their preferred way of thinking. It is a matter of debate among Christians, for example, whether the will of God expressed in the commandments, or the plan of God expressed in structures of creation, or the interaction of God with us in the historic covenants ought to establish a preference among us for one or other of the three. Many today have come to the conclusion that the model of ethical thinking based on interaction is more consistent with the gospel narrative of salvation as a whole. The methods of the law have their uses and wisdom, but need to be interpreted in a wider context. Respect for the integrity and good of the natural or-

Three Styles of Ethical Thinking

	Duty Ethics (Deontological)	**Naturalist Ethics** (Teleological)	**Interactive Ethics**
Key Question	Is this right? Does it obey the rules? Am I being dutiful?	What is good? Does this help achieve the rational natural ends and purposes?	Is this responsible? Is it a constructive response to the relationships and environment?
What makes something "right"?	Actions are in line with the law as established by a legitimate authority.	Actions are valued as good to the extent that they meet the purpose, and fulfil the natural end.	Given the circumstances, it best expresses our values. Actions reflect authentic meaning in relationships and contribute to the ongoing development of mature relationships.
View of God	Authorative law-giver	Architect of purpose through structures of creation.	Interactor through ongoing covenants.
Response to homosexuality	Looks for Biblical command	Looks for purpose and naturalness of the homosexual relationship.	Looks for responsbile and mature relationship.

der is a major concern for us on a global basis. Pursuing short term human goals by cutting down whole rain forests undermines long-term ecological purposes. It is a matter of interpreting these ethics within the ethics of responsibility. The *real* meaning of the legal and rational traditions only appears when we ask what is the most creative behavioural response to all the human and environmental relationships that must be honoured in a given set of circumstances.

Jesus was operating on principles like these when he was attacked for healing a woman on the sabbath. He replied, "Does not each of you on the sabbath untie his ox or his donkey from the manger and lead it away to give it water? And ought not this woman ... be set free from this bondage on the sabbath day?" (Luke 13:15f)

Can you apply these methods to the question of the morality of homosexuality and homosexual relationships?

Recognizing these methods makes plain where some of our problems lie in discussing these questions. It is not that any of the methods will necessarily lead to a simple 'yea' or 'nay'. We can use the ethics of duty to argue that homosexual behaviour is wrong because certain biblical passages appear to condemn it; but we could also use it to argue that it can be right because God 'commands' us to love one another. We can argue that homosexual behaviour is bad because the purpose of sexual behaviour is reproduction, and when that end is excluded the activity is unnatural and irrational; or that it is good because it is natural to persons created with sexual orientation to persons of their own gender. Or we can argue that it is responsible or irresponsible depending on the relationships. We will be predisposed to prefer one or other of the methods, or argue in one or other way within that method by factors that lie outside ethics itself, for example, by our life experiences, our culture and tradition, our value commitment, etc. Recognition of the methods enables us to discern the patterns of thinking we, and those with whom we may disagree, are using.

Do these different ethical ways of thinking create confusion in discussions of moral behaviour?

They do when they are not recognized. People making moral claims that certain actions are right or wrong don't always realize that they and their discussion partners may be using different ethical languages and logics. They may use the same words, but the words carry different weights and tones; their arguments are not being conducted according to the same rules. No wonder it often produces a 'dialogue of the deaf'. Only when you know your own preferred method of ethical thinking, and that of your discussion partner, do you have much chance of really communicating and not just talking at and past one another.

The Rev. Tom Mabey teaches at the Atlantic School of Theology and is the ecumenical partner on the Task Force on Homosexuality and Homosexual Relationships.

SESSION FOUR 56

Seeking Understanding in our Ethical Decisions

OBJECTIVE:

To rebuild the group; to review Our Group Standards.

 Time: 15 minutes

SESSION GOALS

- To examine how the Bible is used to make ethical decisions.
- To identify how ethical positions about homosexuality and homosexual relationships are reached.
- To recognize the diversity of ethical positions.

GATHERING

REBUILDING THE GROUP

As a way of rebuilding the learning community, ask the participants:

What, for you, were the highlights of the previous sessions?

Have you had any new insights since the last session?

PRAYER

Choose a prayer from the Worship Resources, p. 87.

Say together a prayer chosen from the Worship Resources.

Run video (1 minute)

SESSION INTRODUCTION AND REVIEW OF OUR GROUP STANDARDS

SESSION FOUR

OBJECTIVE:

To examine how the Bible is used to make ethical decisions.

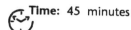
Time: 45 minutes

Ask four participants to read aloud the following preamble and passages.

THINKING ABOUT ETHICS

BIBLE STUDY AND REFLECTION

VOICE 1: PREAMBLE

Human beings were created to live responsibly in contexts of intimate relationship. The creation story in Genesis 1 focussed on human identity in relationship to God. The following passage from Genesis 2 focuses on human identity in relationship to other creatures and ultimately on an ideal of intimate relationship with one another. The passage from Mark 10 addresses a question that arises when that ideal begins to break down.

Working individually, choose one or more passages from the handout. Then read the passage(s) you have chosen and circle the words or short phrases which, for you, point to the key moral message of the passage.

VOICE 2: GENESIS 2:18-25

¹⁸The Lord God said, "It is not good that the man should be alone; I will make him a helper as his partner." ¹⁹So out of the ground the Lord God formed every animal of the field and every bird of the air, and brought them to the man to see what he would call them; and whatever the man called every living creature, that was its name. ²⁰The man gave names to all cattle, and to the birds of the air, and to every animal of the field; but for the man there was not found a helper as his partners. ²¹So the Lord God caused a deep sleep to fall upon the man, and he slept; then he took one of his ribs and closed up its place with flesh. ²²And the rib that the Lord God had taken from the man he made into a woman and brought her to the man. ²³Then the man said, "This at last is bone of my bones, and flesh of my flesh; this one shall be called Woman, for out of Man this one was taken." ²⁴Therefore a man leaves his father and his mother and clings to his wife, and they become one flesh. ²⁵And the man and his wife were both naked, and were not ashamed.

VOICE 3: MARK 10:1-12

¹He left that place and went to a region of Judea and beyond the Jordan. And crowds again gathered around him; and, as was his custom, he again taught them. ²Some Pharisees came, and to test him they asked, "Is it lawful for a man to divorce his wife?" ³He answered them, "What did Moses command you?" ⁴They said, "Moses allowed a man to write a certificate of dismissal and to divorce her." ⁵But Jesus said to them, "Because of your hardness of heart he wrote this commandment for you. ⁶But from the beginning of

creation, 'God made them male and female'. ⁷"For this reason a man shall leave his father and mother ⁸and be joined to his wife, and the two shall become one flesh.' So they are no longer two, but one flesh. ⁹Therefore what God has joined together, let no one separate." ¹⁰Then in the house the disciples asked him again about this matter. ¹¹He said to them, "Whoever divorces his wife and marries another commits adultery against her, ¹²and if she divorces her husband and marries another, she commits adultery."

Voice 4: Mark 12:28-31

²⁸One of the scribes came near and heard them disputing with one another, and seeing that he answered them well, he asked him, "Which commandment is the first of all?" ²⁹Jesus answered, "The first is, 'Hear, O Israel: the Lord our God, the Lord is one; ³⁰you shall love the Lord your God with all your heart, and with all your soul, and with all your mind, and with all your strength.' ³¹The second is this, 'You shall love your neighbour as yourself.' There is no other commandment greater than these."

Individual reflection

Working individually, remind the participants that they are to choose one or two passages and circle the words or short phrases that, for them, point to the key moral message of the passage.

When all have finished writing, ask the participants to form small groups

In the whole group

In the reading for this session, *A Conversation on Ethics*, the Rev. Tom Mabey identifies three modes of ethical decision-making:
- **rules or law,**
- **the right or natural order of things,**
- **the quality of responsible relationships.**

Looking at the words or phrases you highlighted in the Bible passages, how do these passages speak to you about these modes of decision-making?

Have you ever made any decision in your life which was based on the reasoning found in any of these passages? How so?

Have you ever felt any tension in choosing to make, or not make, a decision because of the reasoning found in any of these passages? How so?

What other factors influence your ethical decision-making?

Gather on newsprint the list of factors which influence our ethical decision-making.

Break

10 minutes

SESSION FOUR

OBJECTIVE:

To identify how ethical positions about homosexuality and homosexual relationships are reached; to recognize the diversity of ethical positions.

Time: 40 minutes

As leader, choose one of the following three stories for the group to discuss

or

Ask the participants to form three groups and give each group a different story.

Ask participants to form 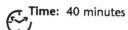 small groups, read the story and discuss the questions found at the end of the text.

PERSONAL EXPERIENCES OF ETHICAL DECISION-MAKING

A REFLECTION FROM A PRIEST

I approach the issue of homosexuality as one whose sexual orientation seems predominantly homosexual, and also as one who desires to be faithful to the overall revelation and intent of the scriptures, as I understand them. Not an easy combination.

As I read the Bible, I find very positive teachings concerning God's creative intention for sexuality. I find that heterosexual marriage is a gift from God. At the same time I read that heterosexuality itself is fallen, and is in need of redemption and healing.

Concerning homosexual behaviour, I find no teaching promoting or blessing homosexual union, either in the Old or New Testaments. And several texts indicate that, at the very least, homosexual union falls short of God's intention. For me, the overwhelming scriptural 'promotion' of healed and redeemed heterosexuality, and the lack of positive mention of homosexuality, speaks even louder than the relatively few prohibitive texts.

There have been times in my life when I have wanted to find biblical sanction for homosexual relationship. But in my conscience, and from my intellect, I simply do not believe a biblical case can be made for such a sanction.

On issues such as divorce, and the ordination of women, I believe that there are sufficient scriptural principles on which to arrive at a biblical position which allows divorce (and remarriage), and promotes the ordination of women. Rightly or wrongly, I believe that there is such scriptural warrant, which does *justice to the texts*. But I find no such principles concerning homosexuality as a way of life. And to proceed without reference to scripture would, I believe, be disastrous.

It is true that the scripture does not seem to speak in terms of homosexual orientation, but simply of homosexual behaviour. The apostle Paul's reference to "such were some of you" (I Cor. 6:11) refers at least to change in behaviour patterns. But perhaps there is here also the seed of a deeper change. Though nobody knows all of the intricate influences on the development of a homosexual orientation, many homosexual Christians have experienced healing of "ancient" wounds in the context of a loving Christian support group of people with similar goals.

I despise the way some preachers use texts of scripture to humiliate and to alienate those who have a homosexual orientation. I shudder at "gay jokes" so thoughtlessly circulated in some church settings, knowing the

SESSION FOUR 60

hurt that they will engender in some. I reject the way some make a "holy crusade" against homosexuality as if it were the chief cause of the world's ills.

At the same time, I worry that in some circles it is "ecclesiastically incorrect" for a Christian to express hope for change either in their homosexual lifestyle, or their orientation, or both. The journey for homosexual Christians who do not believe that a homosexual lifestyle is God's call is difficult and lonely enough without the Church telling them that their quest is useless, foolish, or 'fundamentalist'. In my own journey, I have found that some in the church are rejecting of fellow Christians simply on the basis of orientation, quite apart from lifestyle. Still others are scandalized by a Christian homosexual who does not believe that it is the will of God to act out his or her sexual orientation.

I do not believe that the church should bless homosexuality at the very moment when there are secular and Christian voices pointing to new possibilities of change. And if we are going to call people to a biblical lifestyle either of celibacy or heterosexual marriage, we must also be communities of faith in which people are supported, and loved over time, and shown great patience and powerful prayer along the way. This may involve a type of suffering. But Christians have never been strangers to the suffering which is a by-product of desiring to live in a way which pleases God.

QUESTIONS:

 This writer addresses a process where ethical decision-making is linked to action or behaviour. In small groups, consider the story you have just read and reflect upon...
- What were the ethical or moral decisions?
- In what ways is the person struggling with a call to:
  - Be obedient to rules or laws of God and/or the Church;
  - Follow a natural or right relationship as designed by God;
  - Put relationships with people into an order that reflects the love of God.
- Where are the struggles?
- Are there ways in which this kind of ethical reasoning is familiar to you and your style of making decisions?
- Are there ways that it doesn't fit?

AN EASTER STORY

About two years ago I went to a crucifixion. It took place in the intensive care unit at the hospital where I was in training for hospital chaplaincy. This twentieth-century crucifixion was a bitter-sweet reminder for me of the mystery of the cross, whose power can only be experienced and never understood.

The story began on a Sunday, the first day of what was to become an extraordinary Holy Week. In the midst of a routine visit to the intensive care unit, I noticed a patient sitting up in his bed eating his dinner. I noticed him for three reasons. One, there was the tell-tale fushia sign over his cubicle, the sign containing a list of precautionary directions for hospital workers, the sign that spelled out AIDS for those in the know. Two, this patient was noticeable because he was sitting up. His vertical position seemed unusual in this unit of generally horizontal persuasion. To be in an intensive care unit is to be one who needs to lie down, not sit up. And three, I noticed him because he was, in a word, as my daughters would have put it, a "hunk". He was one of the most beautiful young men I've ever seen. He was tall and dark skinned, of Puerto Rican extraction, thin but not wasted, fine-boned, with large brown eyes that seemed to look right through you, a head of dark, thick, shiny hair that one would kill for. His manner, his bearing, and his gestures exuded a kind of power and charisma.

He was sitting up eating his supper with some difficulty. In one hand he held an oxygen mask, in the other his fork. He would take a bite of food, chew for a few seconds, and then place the mask over his nose and mouth and breathe deeply for a minute. There was a rhythm to this activity, a focused concentration which seemed to elevate mundane actions to the level of music and dance. He was, I discovered, a dancer and a choreographer.

There was a moment of awkwardness when he looked up to see this strange woman staring at him. Then I introduced myself, apologized for staring, asked if I might come back later, and expressed the fact that I had never seen anyone eat and breathe with so much grace. He smiled, and all my clinical detachment flew out the window. He was somehow in charge of our transaction, and he spoke not a word.

Later, when I returned, his family had arrived. His mother, his father, his brother, and an ex-girlfriend who was now a good friend. It was obvious that his family adored him. He was their shining star, their pride and joy. They stroked his brow, patted his arm, held his hand, smoothed his hair, and murmured sounds of constant encouragement. I glanced through his chart at the nurses' station. Steven, age 30, Roman Catholic. Diagnosis: Pneumocystis Pneumonia. Warning: family not to be told of the patient's condition. Patient also requests not to be put on life-supporting breathing apparatus.

Linda, the girlfriend, drew me aside to explain. "He's only come out as being gay in the last few years, and he doesn't want to disappoint his family. They've always been so close, especially he and his dad, and he knows how orthodox they are in their religious beliefs. Mother Church knows best. So they think he just has some severe pneumonia. He doesn't want them to know he's gay." So I kept quiet.

The next day, Monday, when I went back to the unit, I saw Steven lying flat on his back with a breathing tube down his throat. Apparently, he had awakened in the middle of the night to find himself drowning in his own fluid, and, in a natural reflex of panic, he had requested the tube. Was I never to hear the sound of his voice? His family had all but taken up residence in the waiting room. Night and day, they visited him in his cubicle, together and in shifts. Faithful disciples tending to this special son. I thought of the many people with AIDS lying in loneliness with no one to soothe their fevered brows, no one for whom they might be shining stars. But then, Steven's parents believed that he only had a difficult pneumonia from which he would surely recover. After all, he was a dancer, young, in good physical condition, and so full of power and natural magnetism, on the brink of so much success. He was a fighter. He had the will, the grace, and the talent. Steven communicated loving notes to his family with his pencil and a large yellow pad.

By Wednesday night, however, his condition was deteriorating. He was weaker, his handwriting less sure. The tubes attached to his body seemed to multiply. Morphine was added to his medication program. Steven's mother decided it was time to call in some outside specialist to look into the matter. The hospital doctors didn't seem to be helping. Linda was feeling the burden of the secret knowledge which couldn't be revealed. The doctor confided to me his sense that Steven would probably not make it through the week. His body was beginning to bloat from kidney malfunctioning. His vital signs were weakening. His mother called the specialist.

Linda could bear the burden no longer. She confronted Steven early Thursday morning. "Please tell them" she said. "You're not being fair to them or to yourself. They will probably find out anyway after you're gone. There are papers to sign which name this disease. And then they will be left having to deal with an important aspect of you with only a grave to talk to. Don't let them go through this alone. Don't hold back from them such a vital part of you. Do this for them and trust the love that exists between you." Steven wrote on his pad with great effort: "I'll think about it."

All that Thursday Steven lay in his garden of Gethsemane, his garden lush with tubes and machines and plastic bags. He could not speak to us of his struggle, he was too weak to write all his thoughts on that yellow pad. I dared not suggest that the truth would set everyone free, for I would not be paying the price. This was between Steven and his God. It was his choice to make, his risk to take.

Friday morning Steven's pad contained the following words: "I have AIDS. I am Gay." No amount of morphine could have dulled the pain of that day. His mother stood by him, her love never wavered, but she knew now that he would die. His brother stayed also, though we never knew what he thought. But his father was angry, his anger fashioned a cross for Steven. His words cut into Steven's flesh like the stinging thongs of a scourging whip, like nails piercing skin and muscle and nerve tissue, like the sharp points of thorns digging into the head, sending acute laser-like pains throughout the face and deep into the ears. "You brought this disease upon yourself. It is God's judgement for your sin. I have no sons who are fags, and so you are not my son. I disown you. You did this to us, and you can rot in hell!" And he walked out. He did not stop to see the new words Steven was laboriously writing on his pad in large shaky letters which could no longer follow the lines. "I love you." Dad was gone. Steven was no longer his father's shining star. He was cast out.

All day Saturday, the father stayed away. And Steven's beauty deteriorated further. He had now no "form or comeliness that we should look at him and no beauty that we should desire him... he was despised and we esteemed him not." Yet his mother, his brother, and Linda stood by. He could not speak to them of his loneliness and despair. He was doing a mighty work of love, and he was doing it by himself. He had chosen this path. Now he could only endure.

On Sunday, the father returned. He remained alone in the cubicle with his son. Later he told us of some of the conversation. "Steven, you have turned my world upside down. All day yesterday, I was angry. All night, I did not sleep. I was angry that you had not told me sooner. I was angry that you told me at all. I was angry because it seemed as though you were making me choose between my moral beliefs and my son, my Church and you. I have been taught that the Church speaks for God and says that being a homosexual is wrong and AIDS is a consequence of Sin. But I love you and so now nothing is clear any more, and I don't know what this disease is saying to me. I wanted you to tell me you were sorry. I do not say that I will ever understand about this Gay business, but you are my son and I know of your goodness. I have memories of our closeness and so I must wrestle with all that you are and to love all that you are, not just the pieces that fit in with my Church's rules. So now I tell you that it is I who am sorry, and I ask your forgiveness." There were tears. There was joy. The rest was all private, the kind of communing that occurs between people who have resolved their differences and are reconciled. It was a Sunday event.

Three hours later Steven slipped into a coma and died. We were all with him, and he died in peace. The father tore off the page from Steven's pad which said, "I have AIDS. I am Gay" and which also said, down at the bottom in large five-year-old letters, "I love you". He folded it carefully and put it in his pocket. The last words of the boy who was, and would remain, his shining star.

QUESTIONS:

 This story tells of an experience where ethical decision-making is linked to action or behaviour. In small groups, consider the story you have just read and reflect upon...

- What were the ethical or moral decisions?

- In what ways did the people in the story struggling with a call to:
  - Be obedient to rules or laws of God and/or the Church;
  - Follow a natural or right relationship as designed by God;
  - Put relationships with people into an order that reflects the love of God.

- Do you think that the people, when making these ethical decisions, would see themselves as doing that which is good, right, or responsible? Why? Where are the struggles?

- When a change was made in their behaviour or attitude, do you think that a different ethical decision-making mode was used?

- Are there ways in which the type(s) of ethical decision-making found in this story is familiar to you and your style of making decisions? Are there ways it doesn't fit?

A Woman's Story

In our family, religious training began practically at the cradle. The main lesson was learning "right" from "wrong". By the time we were 12 years old, these lists were very long and immovable. Being gay or even thinking about loving someone of the same sex was definitely on the "Very Wrong" list.

Since I knew I was undoubtedly gay at about 10 years old, I felt caught in a terrible dilemma. If I kept falling in love with other girls or imagined a world where I could, as a grown-up have a wonderful, loving relationship for the rest of my life, I was in serious trouble. If I did these "bad" things, God would be mad at me and punish me with unhappiness (and if I kept it up, send me to hell), and it also meant that I didn't really love God because I was refusing to do the "right" thing.

I tried to like boys for a few years, tried to stop thinking or doing anything "gay", and then gave up hope of ever having a loving relationship for the rest of my life. When I was 28 years old, I abandoned my church, my religious "right/wrong" training, and the God who didn't accept gay relationships. I was gay, I wasn't able to stomp it out of existence, and I simply refused to be alone and unloved all my life. I wasn't about to reveal this change to my family though. Their reactions would not be pleasant.

Time went by, and I found myself in that wonderful, loving relationship with an incredible woman that I had dreamed about at 12. I wanted to share my happiness, my life, and myself with my younger sister, so I watched and listened to everything she said and tried to figure out where she stood on the homosexual issue. Any clues I got from her seemed to indicate that she was in agreement with my old church friend who once said, "I think all homosexuals should just be lined up against a wall and shot". Everything I heard made me believe that my sister would despise me, feel uncomfortable in my presence, and might just cut me right out of her life. So I continued to hide and mislead her, to keep her off-track.

Then, one year ago, my ears began to pick up new messages. My sister was telling me about a girlfriend who did AIDS education and who had lots of gay male friends. I figured this was promising but didn't mean she'd like a gay sister. Then she told me how infuriated she had been when our cousin had been "holding forth" at my parent's home about how God had sent the floods to Mississippi to punish homosexuals. She exclaimed to me: "I think that if someone is gay, they're born that way, and since God made them that way, it can't be wrong." I stopped breathing. This was unbelievable. But still I wasn't absolutely sure I could safely "come out".

She seemed intent on telling me through such code language that I could trust her. She kept up with her campaign. A birthday present she gave me was a book about a mother losing a son to AIDS. She then told me how much she had enjoyed being with the gay men that she'd met. I was finally convinced that my sister would probably not hate me if I told her that I was gay. I chose the moment, grabbed a big breath and gave her the news. I began to share my life story and its joys with her. She was wonderful!

As it turned out, she had been convinced that I was gay for years and had been racking her brains trying to figure out a way to get me to just tell her. That night, she met my partner, and we all went out for dinner. I just sat back and watched their eyes dance with excitement and happiness as they talked together. My relief and joy was indescribable.

I don't expect the same acceptance from the rest of my family — they remain locked up with their lists of "Right" and "Wrong". But I hug on tight to this wonderful, and somewhat unbelievable, experience — my sister knows I'm gay and it's quite okay!!

QUESTIONS:

 This story tells of an experience where ethical decision-making is linked to action or behaviour. In small groups, consider the story you have just read and reflect upon...

- What were the ethical or moral decisions?
- In what ways are the people in the story struggling with a call to:
  - Be obedient to rules or laws of God and/or the Church;
  - Follow a natural or right relationship as designed by God;
  - Put relationships with people into an order that reflects the love of God.
- Do you think that the people, when making these ethical decisions, would see themselves as doing that which is good, right, or responsible?
- Why? Where are the struggles?
- When the person (people) made a change in their behaviour or attitude, did they use a different ethical decision-making mode in making this change.
- Are there ways in which the type(s) of ethical decision-making found in this story is familiar to you and your style of making decisions? Are there ways it doesn't fit?

| Session Four | 67 |

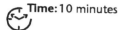
Time: 10 minutes

In the whole group:

Choose a prayer from the Worship Resources, p. 87.

You may wish to prepare for closing by asking the group to stand, gathering into a circle, lighting a candle, observing a few moments of silence.

Closing Worship

Review the newsprint list and add any other factors which influence our ethical decision-making.

Prayer

Say together a closing prayer.

Where to Go From Here

For Further Study

Batchelor, E. **Homosexuality and Ethics.** 1980. New York: Pilgrim Press.

Guindon, A. **The Sexual Creators: An Ethical Proposal for Concerned Christians 1986.** Lanham, MD: University Press of America.

Mollencott, Virginia Ramey: **Sensuous Spirituality: Out from Fundamentalism, 1992.** New York: Crossroads Publications (see especially Appendix B – Diverse Forms of Family Mentioned or Implied in the Hebrew Christian Scriptures).

Pronk, P. **Against Nature? Types of moral argument regarding homosexuality.** 1993. Grand Rapids: Erdmans.

John Spong and John Stott, **Christian Sexual Ethics.** Video, 30 minutes, Anglican Book Centre.

Sojourners, July 1991.

Reading for the Next Session

by the Rev. Dr. George Porter, p. 69

SESSION FOUR	68

 NOTES AND REFLECTIONS

Please read before the next session

It seems that whenever issues around homosexuality and homosexual relationships are raised, there are those who question the possibility of "healing". Some who use the term "healing" are referring to the opportunities to be "cured" from what is perceived by them as an unhealthy orientation. Our Christian tradition speaks a lot about healing and in fact takes on many forms of healing. It is important for our discussions that we not limit our understanding of healing, or assume we all mean the same thing.

Dr. George Porter offers a brief paper to help us identify many of the ways we experience healing within our tradition. We hope that this paper will help us explore the complexity of what "healing" can mean, and help us develop sensitivity when we refer to it in dialogue.

An Exploration of Healing

by the Rev. Dr. George Porter

In the delightful tale *Through the Looking Glass,* Alice objects to the way Humpty Dumpty uses the word 'glory'. He replies: 'When I use a word ... it means just what I choose it to mean — neither more nor less.' To this Alice says: 'The question is ... whether you can make words mean so many different things.'

Humpty Dumpty may be just a comical fictional character, but his approach to words and meanings is not something unfamiliar to contemporary society. Despite the objections of Alice, words are often made to mean just what their speaker or writer chooses. There are many ways to understand even very common terms.

When the term 'healing' appears in dialogue about homosexuality and homosexual relationships, one cannot simply assume that everyone assigns it the same meaning. Rather, it may signify a number of different things to different people. One who attempts to hear what various people are saying in this regard must be careful to try to discern how the word is being used.

How 'healing' is used by various individuals really depends to a large degree upon how a particular individual understands the origins of sexual orientation (aetiology), as well as the possibility or desirability of changing orientation. A significant number of understandings are represented within the membership of the Anglican Church of Canada.

For some, healing for gay and lesbian people means reversing their sexual orientation. From this perspective, homosexuality may be viewed as either sinful or pathological (medically, morally, or psycho-socially disordered).

On the one hand, if this orientation is believed to be sinful, originating in some way with wilful choice on the part of individuals, what would be required in the process of healing would be confession, repentance and new choices of sexual direction. Many who call themselves 'ex-gays' or 'former homosexuals' hold this belief.

On the other hand, if homosexuality is believed to be pathological, resulting from forces beyond a person's conscious control, some form of therapy designed to enable one to change his/her sexual orientation would be called for. In the past, attempts at changing sexual orientation have involved a variety of surgical procedures, drug administration or hormonal treatments. Currently this might involve healing prayer, counselling, psychotherapy, hypnotherapy or behaviour modification techniques. Some refer to themselves as 'recovering gays/lesbians.'

Related to these ideas are the beliefs that homosexuality is either an addictive behaviour, similar to alcoholism, or a handicap. In either case, healing involves avoiding homosexual relationships and behaviours which would be seen as reinforcing the addiction or complicating the handicap. Healing is learning to live within the unchangeable limitation placed upon one by life, regardless of the origins of those limitations. Within this context, some believe that they can meaningfully accept and affirm themselves as gay and lesbian persons while choosing not to express their intimacy in genital acts.

In line with this, many others insist that a distinction must be made between sexual orientation and sexual behaviour. From this perspective, change of orientation may not be possible and is not necessary. The orientation, whatever its origins may be, is not regarded as culpable. Only homosexual acts are seen as problematic.

Healing, therefore, would not require a person to change his/her sexual orientation. It would mean gay men or lesbians choosing not to engage in physical acts of sexual intimacy. Essentially, the only option left for gay and lesbian people would be celibacy (sexual abstinence).

Another point of view concerning the origins of homosexual orientation sees it as a relational dysfunction. This may take the form of understanding it as being the result of abuse, especially sexual abuse, or circumstantial influences (e.g. single sex institutions such as schools, prisons or the military).

More commonly it involves the belief that a homosexual orientation emerges in the context of dysfunctional family relationships. Formerly, under Freudian influence, this was understood primarily as conflict and distance between a person and his/her opposite sex parent. More recently it has been understood as conflict and/or distance between a person and his/her same-sex parent. Homosexuality is seen, therefore, as being not really a sexual orientation but as either compensation or defensive reaction.

In either case, healing cannot be understood properly as 'reorientation' or 'orientation conversion'. Healing involves not focusing on sexual manifestations but sorting out the dysfunctional relationship web from which these expressions arise. When once this dysfunctional web is identified and disentangled, the question of homosexual identity is believed to gradually resolve itself.

Another approach is taken by those who do not accept homosexual relationships as equal to heterosexual relationships but realize that neither of the alternatives (orientation change or celibacy) appears to be possible for some gay and lesbian people. Healing, in this understanding, would involve a pastoral affirmation of some homosexual relationships involving standards of commitment and integrity such as those proposed by H. Norman Pittenger.

Not all approaches to healing, however, place homosexuality in a negative understanding. For others, healing involves some sense of affirmation or self-affirmation of gay and lesbian people and relationships.

Some speak of 'coming out' as a healing event. A gay man or lesbian comes at some point to recognize and accept his/her sexual orientation as a reality, and ultimately a positive reality. S/he comes out to her/him self. Gradually s/he shares this experience with others. This can be experienced as liberating; s/he is finally free of secrecy and pretending. It can also be an experience of rejection and, therefore, of loss. It can be a paradox of healing and wounding.

As stories of gay and lesbian people are told, many kinds of wounding and pain emerge, especially the pain of rejection and exclusion. Healing has meaning here as well. Although the HIV/AIDS factor is not a specifically homosexual phenomenon, many homosexual persons have died and are dying from complications resulting from this virus. The physical suffering, relational pain and socioeconomic hardships related to this actuality must involve healing.

Healing is not, in this sense, equated with cure. Healing involves restoring some measure of wholeness to persons who have been wounded in various ways.

Healing could then also involve two further steps. One might be attempting to resolve the rejection through reconciliation. Alternatively, one might also be faced with moving through a grief process where such losses as cannot be healed through reconciliation are resolved.

Healing involving experiences of loss may involve other aspects of life as well. HIV/AIDS has already been mentioned in this regard. Loss can also involve loss of potential (e.g. having one's own children, exclusion from certain career choices). The grieving process can make a contribution to resolving these ordeals as well.

Living in secrecy, denial and pretension often contributes to emotional and relational complications for gay and lesbian people. Among such complications can be a lack of accurate sense of value or low self-esteem. Counselling would focus on healing as strengthening self-esteem. Healing would mean that a gay man or lesbian would be able to see him/herself as a person of value and experience the love and esteem of others.

Gay and lesbian people generally experience many of the same kinds of relationship and intimacy difficulties as do those involved in heterosexual relationships. Healing involves sorting these out and learning to live together. Some believe that lack of social support structures and positive role models for relationships contributes to greater difficulty among gay and lesbian people of making commitments and forming long-lasting relationships. Healing would necessarily involve resolving those issues as well. Sharing by gay men and lesbians who have entered into and maintained committed relationships is seen as a major contributing factor in this type of healing process.

Healing is not, however, only to be understood in an exclusively individualistic sense. Many also believe that healing involves issues of justice: our social networks and institutions, (including our own church).

Voices from many directions in the church call for healing of irrational fear of, and hostility toward, gay and lesbian people (sometimes called 'homophobia'). Most people recognize the need for repentance from such attitudes of hostility, exclusion and even persecution of gay men and lesbians.

For some that means some type of qualified acceptance of gay and lesbian persons, and open and honest support for those either wanting to live in celibacy or seeking orientation change, without affirming homosexual relationships. This seems to be very much in line with recent statements by the Church of England House of Bishops.

Others believe that healing must involve an unqualified acceptance of gay and lesbian people, as well as recognition and affirmation of committed same-gender relationships. Essentially this involves applying the same standards to both homosexual and heterosexual relationships. Anything less is seen as simply continuing, if in a less obvious form, the present conditions. Anything less is seen as trying a band-aid approach which is not really healing.

These approaches and understandings, and many other variations, of healing for gay and lesbian people are all present in the Anglican Church of Canada. The question remains of how to avoid a hopeless Humpty Dumpty situation with so many different potential meanings. A genuine consensus about the meaning of healing is unlikely. At the very least, however, meaningful dialogue around homosexuality and homosexual relationships in the church requires that we have some understanding of the various ways that this term may be being used.

The Rev. Dr. George Porter, Diocese of Brandon, Manitoba, is a member of the General Synod Task Force on Homosexuality and Homosexual Relationships.

SESSION FIVE — 5

Living Out Our Baptismal Covenant

OBJECTIVE:

To rebuild the group; to review Our Group Standards

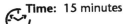
Time: 15 minutes

SESSION GOALS

- To hear and reflect on different experiences of lesbian and gay people in the Anglican Church of Canada.
- To reflect on personal experiences of inclusion and exclusion.
- To look at ways our community can be inviting and inclusive.

GATHERING

REBUILDING THE GROUP

Recite together the Baptismal Covenant (from the *Book of Alternative Services*, page 158-159).

THE BAPTISMAL COVENANT

Do you believe in God the Father?
**I believe in God
the Father almighty,
creator of heaven and earth.**

Do you believe in Jesus Christ, the Son of God?

**I believe in Jesus Christ,
his only Son, our Lord.
He was conceived by the power of the Holy Spirit
and born of the Virgin Mary.
He suffered under Pontius Pilate,
was crucified, died, and was buried.
He descended to the dead.
On the third day he rose again.
He ascended into heaven,
and is seated at the right hand of the Father.
He will come again to judge the living and the dead.**

SESSION FIVE

Do you believe in God the Holy Spirit?

**I believe in God the Holy Spirit,
the holy catholic Church,
the communion of saints,
the forgiveness of sins,
the resurrection of the body,
and the life everlasting.**

Will you continue in the apostles' teaching and fellowship, in the breaking of bread, and in the prayers?

I will, with God's help.

Will you persevere in resisting evil and, whenever you fall into sin, repent and return to the Lord?

I will, with God's help.

Will you proclaim by word and example the good news of God in Christ?

I will, with God's help.

Will you seek and serve Christ in all persons, loving your neighbour as yourself?

I will, with God's help.

Will you strive for justice and peace among all people, and respect the dignity of every human being?

I will, with God's help.

Ask the participants to share...

As you reflect on the past week are there ways in which you fulfilled the promises of the Baptismal Covenant?

SESSION FIVE 74

Run video (2 minutes)

SESSION INTRODUCTION AND REVIEW OUR GROUP STANDARDS

OBJECTIVE:

To hear and reflect on diverse experiences of lesbian and gay people in the Anglican Church of Canada.

VOICES — HEARING DIVERSE EXPERIENCES

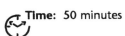 **Time:** 50 minutes

Run video (25 minutes)

Ask the participants to form pairs

HEARING DIVERSE VOICES

Discuss:

What words, phrases, images, or feelings caught your attention?

From what you have just seen and heard, are there common themes?

How are we one communion in the midst of such tension?

BREAK

10 minutes

SESSION FIVE

OBJECTIVE:

To reflect on personal experiences of inclusion and exclusion; to look at ways our community can be inviting and inclusive.

Time: 40 minutes

In the whole group, please read the following statement to the participants

You may wish to dim the lights

Ask the participants to form pairs

Ask the participants to find a comfortable position and close their eyes.

Ask the participants to think about a gathering or group where they felt the discomfort and pain of exclusion.

Ask the participants to resume their comfortable position, close their eyes, then think about a gathering or group where they felt particularly comfortable, and welcome.

In the whole group

EXPLORING OUR CALL TO BE ONE IN CHRIST

PURPOSE

Despite the many different thoughts and feelings about homosexuality and homosexual relationships, lesbian and gay Christians are our sisters and brothers in Christ. We need to recognize those ways we exclude them from our communities and identify ways to become inviting and inclusive.

How does it feel?

How did I know I was excluded?

Share with another participant:

How do I know when I am included?

Brainstorm on newsprint:

What are the characteristics of an inviting community?

| SESSION FIVE | 76 |

Ask the participants to form small groups

Ask the participants to reflect on their own community.

In the whole group

Ask the participants to identify:

Time: 5 minutes
In the whole group

You may wish to prepare for closing by asking the group to stand, gathering into a circle, lighting a candle, observing a few moments of silence.

Ask each participant to add their own words to finish the sentence:

AT HOME IN OUR COMMUNITY

Are there ways we could be more inviting?

Gather all these ideas together on newsprint.

Which of these suggestions do I (or we as a group) have some control over?

Which suggestions would involve working with others?

What action might we want to take? Individually? As a group?

CLOSING WORSHIP

For the good of our community may we...

Conclude each participant's petition with:

**Lord in your Mercy
Hear our prayer.**

SESSION FIVE

WHERE TO GO FROM HERE

FOR FURTHER STUDY

A Study of Human Rights Principles Proposed for the Anglican Church of Canada. 1991. Toronto: Anglican Church of Canada, Human Rights Unit.

Borsch, F. **Christian Discipleship and Human Sexuality.** 1991. Episcopal Diocese of Los Angeles.

Boyd, M. & Wilson, N. (eds.) **Amazing Grace: Stories of Lesbian and Gay Faith.** 1991. The Crossing Press.

Cromey, R.W. **In God's Image.** 1991. San Francisco: Alamo Square Press.

Fortunato, J. **Embracing the Exile: Healing Journeys of Gay Christians.** 1988. San Francisco: Harper and Row.

Glaser, C. **Come Home! Reclaiming Spirituality and Community as Gay Men and Lesbians.** 1990. San Francisco: Harper and Row.

Hilton, B., **Can Homophobia be Cured? Wrestling with Questions that Challenge the Church.** 1992. Nashville, TN: Abingdon.

Howe, J. **Sex: Should We Change the Rules? Let's Argue it out.** 1991. Florida: Creation House.

Selby, P. **Belonging.** 1991. London: SPCK.

Our Stories, Your Story. 1990. Toronto: Anglican Church of Canada

READING FOR NEXT WEEK

Reread Purpose of the Study, p. 6.

| **SESSION FIVE** | 78 | .... |

NOTES AND REFLECTIONS

SESSION SIX

6 Responding as a Community in Christ

OBJECTIVE

To begin to gather the wisdom of the group.

Time: 20 minutes

As a way of rebuilding the learning community, ask the participants:

SESSION GOALS

- To elicit the wisdom of the group to assist our church in making informed and responsible decisions.
- To close the group

GATHERING

REBUILDING THE GROUP

What, for you, were the highlights of the previous session?

Have you had any new insights since the last session?

What have you told other people about your experience with this program of study?

PRAYER

Say responsively

Come, Holy Spirit, creator, and renew the face of the earth.
Come, Holy Spirit, come.

Come, Holy Spirit, counsellor, and touch our lips that we may proclaim your word.
Come, Holy Spirit, come.

Come, Holy Spirit, power from on high: make us agents of peace and ministers of wholeness.
Come, Holy Spirit, come.

Come, Holy Spirit, breath of God, give life to the dry bones of this exiled age, and make us a living people, holy and free.
Come, Holy Spirit, come.

Come, Holy Spirit, wisdom and truth: strengthen us in the risk of faith.
Come, Holy Spirit, come.

[From *The Book of Alternative Services*, p. 123, Anglican Church of Canada]

or

Say together a prayer chosen from the Worship Resources, page 87.

SESSION SIX

Ask for a volunteer to read the preamble and ask participants to take turns reading the verses of the Biblical passage.

REVIEW OF OUR GROUP STANDARDS AND SESSION INTRODUCTION

BIBLE STUDY

PREAMBLE

Paul's first letter the Christians in Corinth is proof against any wide-eyed notions we may have that the first century church was practically perfect in every way. That the Corinthians could have been as mixed up as they were is, in fact, a message that there is hope for us. Among their problems were: the involvement of one member in an incestuous relationship; the indifference of wealthy members to the poverty of others, even at the parish supper that accompanied the eucharist; pride based on charismatic religious experience. We must read chapter 12 of Paul's letter against this all-too credible background. Paul is pleading for unity based on the mutual relationship of very different parts of a living organic body and on recognition that all, even the most gifted, are dependent on the free gift of God's spirit.

1 CORINTHIANS 12:12-21

¹²For just as the body is one and has many members, and all the members of the body, though many, are one body, so it is with Christ.

¹³For in the one Spirit we were all baptized into one body — Jews or Greeks, slaves or free — and we were all made to drink of one Spirit.

¹⁴Indeed, the body does not consist of one member but of many.

¹⁵If the foot would say, "Because I am not a hand, I do not belong to the body," that would not make it any less a part of the body.

¹⁶And if the ear would say, "Because I am not an eye, I do not belong to the body," that would not make it any less a part of the body.

¹⁷If the whole body were an eye, where would the hearing be?

If the whole body were hearing, where would the sense of smell be?

¹⁸But as it is, God arranged the members in the body, each one of them, as he chose.

¹⁹If all were a single member, where would the body be?

²⁰As it is, there are many members, yet one body.

²¹The eye cannot say to the hand, "I have no need of you," nor again the hand to the foot, "I have no need of you."

SESSION SIX

Ask the participants to form small groups.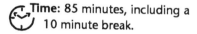

(Ask one member of each group to act as scribe.)

Discuss:

Why do you think Paul chose the image of our body?

What does this imagery teach us about the nature of our Christian community?

What does this imagery teach us about our relationship with each other in the Church?

Gather and record responses on newsprint.

In the whole group

FORMING OUR MESSAGE

OBJECTIVE:

To discern what we want to share with our parish, diocese, and the Anglican Church of Canada.

Time: 85 minutes, including a 10 minute break.

Ask for volunteers to read A Word from the Primate, p. 3, and the Purpose of the Study, p. 6, statement

Individual reflection

In order to help our church more forward to make informed and responsible decisions regarding its future, we are invited to share our voices, our thoughts, feelings and opinions, with the wider church.

Read aloud A Word from the Primate and the Purpose of Study statement.

Take a few minutes on your own to finish the sentences

We have heard many and diverse voices speaking about homosexuality and homosexual relationships

I would like to say...

I say this because...

What questions do you have now about homosexuality and homosexual relationships and the church? Have they changed since you began this program of study?

Session Six

Ask the participants to form pairs

Share with each other

What you have learned from the program of study and from other members of the group.

What you would like to say to the group as a result.

What you would like to say to our church as a result.

Ask two pairs of participants to form groups of four. (Ask one member of each group to act as scribe.)

Discuss:

What do you think this study group has to say to the wider church about the experience with this program of study?

What do you think this study group has to say to the wider church about the issues of homosexuality and homosexual relationships?

BREAK

10 minutes

In the whole group

Gather and record the responses on newsprint.

Looking at these responses we have collected:

Do we, as a group, have a message for our church?

What is our message — our wisdom for the church as it goes forward to make informed and responsible decisions?

Take some time to formulate your message, or delegate the task to a small group.

It will not always be possible to create a message from the whole group. When this is the case, remind the participants that, while they are being invited to respond as a group, individual responses are also welcome.

If this is the case, the group may wish to use this time to formulate their messages as individuals or as small groups using the response form (p. 89). When this is done, move to the Evaluation section.

SESSION SIX

The participants may wish to delegate members of the group to the task of carrying the message(s) forward.

OBJECTIVE:

To evaluate the program of study.

Time: 10 minutes

Please return these evaluation forms and the group's message form as soon as possible.

Time: 5 minutes

Invite each participant to share what they have learned from being a member of the group.

Choose a prayer from the Worship Resources, p. 87.

You may wish to prepare for closing by asking the group to stand, gathering into a circle, lighting a candle, observing a few moments of silence.

Since this is the last session, you may also want to acknowledge the feelings or state of mind of the group. This is especially helpful when the group life has been quite difficult or intimate.

SHARING OUR MESSAGE

With the wider church

If your group wishes to respond to the invitation and send its message to the church, delegate an individual or small group to fill out the form found on page 85. In order to have these responses in time for General Synod 1995, these forms need to be returned **as soon as possible** (see note in Introductory Notes for Facilitators, p. 7).

With others

Does your group wish to share its message(s) with your parish(s) and your diocese.

If so, how?

EVALUATION

Ask participants to fill out the short evaluation form found on page 85 and return them to you before leaving this session.

CLOSING WORSHIP

PRAYER

Say together a closing prayer.

WHERE TO GO FROM HERE

Mollenkott, V., & Scanzoni, L. **Is the Homosexual My Neighbour? Another Christian View.** 1978. San Francisco: Harper and Row.

Reconciling Congregations Program P.O. Box 24213, Nashville, TN. 37202.

| SESSION SIX | 84 |

 **NOTES AND REFLECTIONS**

RESPONSE FORM 85

To send your response, either photocopy this page or remove it from this book.

Our Message to the Church

Parish and Diocese _____

Name of Individual _____

Number in Group _____

Number participating in this message _____

So that we can share our experience and wisdom with the wider church we would like to say:

_____
_____
_____
_____
_____
_____
_____
_____
_____
_____
_____
_____

Please return this form to

THE TASK FORCE ON
HOMOSEXUALITY AND HOMOSEXUAL RELATIONSHIPS
ANGLICAN CHURCH OF CANADA
600 JARVIS STREET
TORONTO, ONTARIO
M4Y 2J6

| EVALUATION | 86 |

To send your response, either photocopy this page or remove it from this book.

Evaluation Form

How much do you feel you have learned from this study:

1　2　3　4　5　6　7　8　9　10

nothing new　　　　　　　　　　　　　　　　many new insights

COMMENT _____

Was the book designed in a way that was helpful and clear?

1　2　3　4　5　6　7　8　9　10

not helpful　　　　　　　　　　　　　　　　very helpful

COMMENT _____

Was the process of the sessions clear and easy to follow?

1　2　3　4　5　6　7　8　9　10

I got completely lost　　　　　　　　　　　　very clear

COMMENT _____

Were the resources provided (readings, videos, bibliography) helpful:

1　2　3　4　5　6　7　8　9　10

not helpful　　　　　　　　　　　　　　　　very helpful

COMMENT _____

Please return this form to

THE TASK FORCE ON HOMOSEXUALITY AND HOMOSEXUAL RELATIONSHIPS
ANGLICAN CHURCH OF CANADA
600 JARVIS STREET
TORONTO, ONTARIO
M4Y 2J6

Three highlights of this program of study were:

1. _____
2. _____
3. _____

If you were to lead this course, what would you do differently? ____
_____

Were you a ☐ facilitator or ☐ participant?

Name: (optional) _____

Parish/Diocese: _____

Worship Resources

HYMNS

Come down O love divine
(Red 67; Blue 487)

God who hast caused to be written
(R99)

Lord of all hopefulness
(R262; B634)

Love divine all loves excelling
(R241; B470)

Now thank we God for bodies strong (R204)

O thou who camest from above
(R239)

Take my life and let it be (R294; B576)

PRAYERS

Preserve us O Lord, in all our doings with thy most gracious favour, and further us with thy continual help; that in all our works begun, continued, and ended in thee, we may glorify thy holy name, and finally by thy mercy obtain everlasting life; through Jesus Christ our Lord. Amen.

(Collect from the Ordinal — Book of Common Prayer)

God of pilgrims, teach us to recognize your dwelling-place in the love, generosity, and support of those with whom we share our journey, and help us to worship you in our response to those who need our care; for all the world is your temple and every human heart is a sign of your presence, made known to us in Jesus Christ our Lord.

(Prayer for Psalm 84, Book of Alternative Services p. 818)

Glorious God, you have taught us in our Saviour Jesus Christ that you are present wherever there is love, and that two or three who gather in his name are citizens of your eternal city. Feed us with the bread of life, that we may grow to recognize in every human heart a sign of your presence and an opportunity to serve you. We ask this in the name of Jesus Christ our Lord.

Amen.

(Prayer for Psalm 132, BAS p. 890)

Creator of the universe, from whom all things come, to whom all things return, give your people such unity of heart and mind, that all the world may grow in the life of your eternal kingdom, through Jesus Christ our Lord.

Amen.

(Prayer for Psalm 133, BAS p. 891)

God of mystery and power, even our minds and hearts are the veils and signs of your presence. We come in silent wonder to learn the way of simplicity, the eternal road that leads to love for you and for your whole creation. We come as your Son Jesus Christ taught us, and in his name.

Amen.

(Prayer for Psalm 139, BAS p. 898)

God of the universe, Lord of life, give us grace to see you in all your works, in all creatures, all people, and in our hearts, that we may faithfully serve you and worthily praise your holy name, through Jesus Christ our Lord.

Amen.

(Prayer for Psalm 147, BAS p. 907)

O God our defender, storms rage about us and cause us to be afraid. Rescue your people from despair, deliver your sons and daughters from fear, and preserve us all from unbelief; through your Son, Jesus Christ our Lord, who lives and reigns with you and the Holy Spirit, one God, now and ever.

Amen.

(Collect for Proper 12, BAS p. 363)

Eternal God, you create us by your power and redeem us by your love. Guide and strengthen us by your Spirit, that we may give ourselves today in love and service to one another and to you; through Jesus Christ our Lord.

Amen.

(A Prayer for strength, BAS p. 130)

Creator of all we see and know, grant us the grace to open our eyes to your living presence in all people and in the world you have created. Help us to lead others in discovery of you so that we all learn and are fed by the many ways you reveal yourself to us.

Amen.

(from Things Too Wonderful: A Manual for the Study and Use of Inclusive Language)

God of tenderness and strength, you have brought our paths together and led us to this day; so be with us now as we travel through good times, through trouble, or through change. Bless our homes, our partings and our meetings.

Make us worthy of each other's best, and tender with each other's dreams, trusting in your love in Jesus Christ.
Amen.

(from A New Zealand Prayer Book)

RESOURCES

Praise be to God who has given us life.
Blessed be God for the gift of love.
Praise to God who forgives our sin.
Blessed be God who sets us free.
Praise to God who kindles our faith.
Blessed be God, our strength, our hope.

(from A New Zealand Prayer Book)

God of peace,
your love is generous,
and reaches out to hold us in your embrace.
Fill our hearts with tenderness
for those to whom we are linked today.
Give us sympathy with each other's trials;
give us patience with each other's faults;
that we may grow in the likeness of Jesus
and share in the joy of your kingdom.
Amen.

(from A New Zealand Prayer Book)

God our Creator,
when you speak there is light and life,
when you act there is justice and love;
grant that your love may be present in our meeting,
so that what we say and what we do
may be filled with your Holy Spirit.
Amen.

[from the New Zealand Prayer Book]

We give you thanks, Spirit of Wisdom,
for you speak to us in ways that often surprise us.
You uncover truths that we have kept hidden from ourselves,
and support us in tasks we fear to undertake alone.
We give thanks for your invitations to growth and intimacy and fullness of life,
and for the comfort you extend in our often uphill struggle to be faithful.
Amen.

[From More Than Words by Janet Schaffran and Pat Kozak]

Closing worship suggestions

A

Dear God,
thank you for all that is good,
for our creation and our humanity,
for the stewardship you have given us of this planet earth,
for the gifts of life and of one another,
for your love which is unbounded and eternal.
O thou, most holy and beloved,
my Companion, my Guide upon the way,
my bright evening star.
We repent of the wrongs we have done:
silence
Amen.

(from A New Zealand Prayer Book)

B

We have wounded your Love
O God, heal us.
We stumble in the darkness.
Light of the world transfigure us.
We forget that we are your home.
Spirit of God dwell in us.
Eternal spirit, living God,
in whom we live and move and have our being,
all that we are, all that we have been,
and all that we shall be is known to you,
to the very secret of our hearts
and all that rises to trouble us.
Living flame, burn into us,
cleansing wind, blow through us,
fountain of water, well us within us,
that we may love and praise in deed and in truth.
Amen.

(from A New Zealand Prayer Book)

C

Let us be at peace within ourselves.
silence
Let us be aware that we are profoundly loved and need never be afraid.
silence
Let us be aware of the source of being that is common to us all and to all living creatures.
silence
Let us be filled with the presence of the great compassion towards ourselves and towards all living beings.
silence
Realizing that we are all nourished from the same source of life, may we so live that others be not deprived of air, food, water, shelter, or the chance to love.
silence
Let us pray that we ourselves cease to be a cause of suffering to one another.
silence
With humility let us pray for the establishment of peace in our hearts and on earth.
silence
May God kindle in us the fire of love, to bring us alive and give warmth to the world.
Amen.

(from A New Zealand Prayer Book)

D

The leader divides the group into two;

the sections are read alternating, first one half, then the other

All: A new commandment I give to you, that you love one another as I have loved you.

1: I have loved you just as the Father has loved me. Remain in my love.

2: If you keep my commandments you will remain in my love, just as I have kept my father's commandments and remain in his love.

All: A new commandment I give to you, that you love one another as I have loved you.

1: I have told you this that my own joy may be in you and your joy be complete.

2: This is my commandment: love one another as I have loved you.

All: A new commandment I give to you, that you love one another as I have loved you.

1: No one can have greater love than to lay down his life for his friends.

2: You are my friends, if you do what I command you.

All: A new commandment I give to you, that you love one another as I have loved you.

1: I shall no longer call you servants, because a servant does not know his master's business; I call you friends because I have made known to you everything I have learnt from my Father.

2: You did not choose me, no, I chose you; and I commissioned you to go out and bear fruit, fruit that will last;

All: A new commandment I give to you, that you love one another as I have loved you.

1: so that the Father will give you anything you ask him in my name.

2: My command to you is to love one another.

(From John 15:9-17)

E

Spend a few moments thinking of the relationships, past and present, that have been important in your life.

Write down a brief statement or prayer of thanks for one or more of these relationships.

Standing together in a circle, everyone may read out their petitions — prayers.

Hymn:

How sweet the name of Jesus sounds (B490; R116)

The blessing of God,
the eternal goodwill of God,
the shalom of God,
the wildness and warmth of God,
be among us and between us,
now and always, Amen.

(prayer from A New Zealand Prayer Book)

F

Keep a few moments of silence while everyone considers how they would complete the sentence

I believe in the God who...

Gather in a circle and a co-leader will begin the closing worship with the following prayer:

Praise to you, God, for all your work among us.
Yours is the vigour in creation.
Yours in the impulse in our new discoveries.
Make us adventurous, yet reverent and hopeful in all we do.

Allow the opportunity for each person to complete her/his sentence. (Let participants know that they may pass if they wish.)

I believe in the God who...

When everyone has finished you may say this doxology:

Glory to God
whose power, working in us,
can do infinitely more than we can ask or imagine.
Glory to God from generation to generation
in the church and in Christ Jesus for ever and ever.
Amen.

(Ephesians 3:20-21)

G

Leader: Let us pray to God the Holy Spirit saying, "Come, Holy Spirit, come."
Come Holy Spirit, creator, and renew the face of the earth.
Come, Holy Spirit Come

Come, Holy Spirit, counsellor, and touch our lips that we may proclaim you word.
Come, Holy Spirit Come

Come, Holy Spirit, power from on high: Make us agents of peace and ministers of wholeness.
Come, Holy Spirit Come

Come Holy Spirit, breath of God, give life to the dry bones of this exiled age, and make us a living people, holy and free.
Come, Holy Spirit Come

Come, Holy Spirit, wisdom and truth: strengthen us in the risk of faith.
Come, Holy Spirit Come

H

Leader: Let us give thanks to God, always and for everything, saying, "We thank you, Gracious God."
For the beauty and wonder of creation,
We thank you, Gracious God.
For all that is gracious in the lives of men and women, revealing the image of Christ,
We thank you, Gracious God.

For minds to think and hearts to love,
We thank you, Gracious God.

For ever-new understandings of who you are ... (here participants may add their own thanksgivings ...)
We thank you, Gracious God.

All may say together:
Blessed are you
God of growth and discovery;
yours is the inspiration
that has altered and changed our lives;
yours is the power that has brought us
to new dangers and opportunities.
Set us, your new creation,
to walk through this new world,
watching and learning,
loving and trusting,
until your kingdom comes.
Amen.

Leader: The Peace of the Lord be always with you
All: And also with you.
People may greet each other in the name of the Lord.

I

Song

We are one in the Spirit, We are one in the Lord,
We are one in the Spirit, We are one in the Lord,
And we pray that all unity may one day be restored
And they'll know we are Christians by our Love, by our Love,
Yes, they'll know we are Christians by our Love.
We will walk with each other, We will walk hand in hand,
We will walk with each other, We will walk hand in hand,
And together we'll spread the news that God is in our land.
And they'll know ...
We will work with each other, We will work side by side,
We will work with each other, We will work side by side,
And we'll guard each other's dignity and save each another's pride,
And they'll know ...
All praise to the Father, From whom all things come,
And all praise to Christ Jesus, His only Son,
And all praise to the Spirit, who makes us one,
And they'll know ...

Designer of the universe, you have created a world of many colours and callings. We delight in your gift of diversity. Teach us to reflect this abundance as a blessing in our faith communities. Help us to appreciate the wealth of possibility and to still our fear of otherness.

Amen.

(from **Things Too Wonderful: A Manual for the Study and Use of Inclusive Language**).

| RESOURCES | 96 | ....

 **NOTES AND REFLECTIONS**